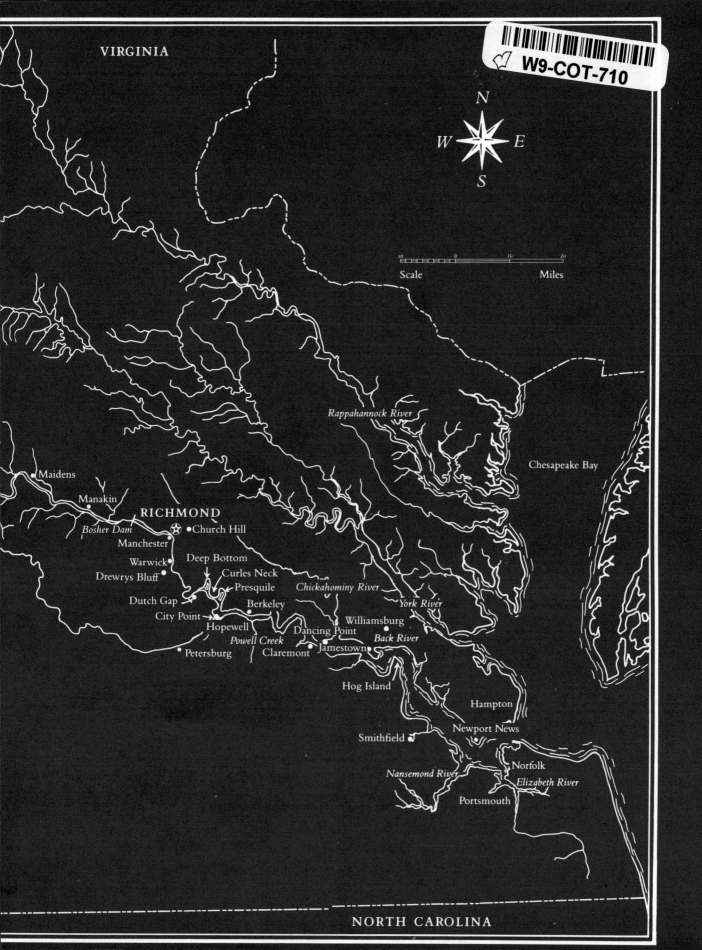

VIRGINIA

N
W E
S

Scale   Miles

Rappahannock River

Chesapeake Bay

Maidens

Manakin

RICHMOND
Bosher Dam   ●Church Hill
Manchester
Warwick   Deep Bottom
Drewrys Bluff   Curles Neck
      Presquile   Chickahominy River
Dutch Gap   Berkeley   York River
City Point
Hopewell   Williamsburg
      Dancing Point   Back River
Powell Creek
Petersburg   Claremont   Jamestown

Hog Island

Hampton

Newport News

Smithfield

Norfolk
Nansemond River   Elizabeth River
Portsmouth

NORTH CAROLINA

IN RIVER TIME

IN RIVER TIME
THE WAY OF THE JAMES

ANN WOODLIEF

with a photographic interpretation
by John Theilgard

ALGONQUIN BOOKS OF CHAPEL HILL

1985

Algonquin Books of Chapel Hill
Post Office Box 2225
Chapel Hill, North Carolina, 27515-2225

ISBN 0-912697-16-4

Permission to reprint lines from T. S. Eliot's "The Dry Salvages" has been granted by Harcourt Brace Jovanovich.
For permission to reproduce illustrations included in this book, the author and publishers wish to express their gratitude to the following:

For permission to reproduce illustrations included in this book, the author and publishers wish to express their gratitude to the following:
Richmond Newspapers, Inc., for photographs of James River in flood, the James River at Balcony Falls, pollution sign on lower James River, Allied Chemical plant at Hopewell, and Newport News Shipbuilding and Dry Dock Company.
Valentine Museum, Richmond, Virginia, for photographs of rope ferry, Dunlap Mills, steamer *Pocahontas*, painting by George W. Cooke, James River during 1930s, and C&O tracks in flood.
John Theilgard, for photographs of Iron Gate and Shirley Plantation.
Virginia State Library, Richmond, Virginia, for photographs of prints of Indians at work on dugout canoe, Captain John Smith threatens Opechancanough, Indian massacre of 1622; James River Canal watercolor by Edward Beyer, Richmond from Gamble's Hill by Edward Beyer; print of the Monitor driving off the Merrimac.
Scottsville Museum, Scottsville, Virginia, for photograph of Horseshoe Bend.
Mariner's Museum, Newport News, Virginia, for photograph of drawing of Amherst Heights by Edward Beyer.
U.S. Army Corps of Engineers, for photograph of Gathright Dam.
Lyn Woodlief, for photographs of pollution and beauty and Falls of the James today.

The author also wishes to express her gratitude to the following museums and libraries for their assistance: Scottsville Museum, Valentine Museum, Virginia Commonwealth University library, Virginia Historical library, Virginia State library.

LIBRARY OF CONGRESS CATALOGING IN PUBLICATION DATA
Woodlief, Ann, 1940–
In river time.
Bibliography: p.   Includes index.
1. James River (Va.)—History.   2. James River
Valley (Va.)—History.   3. James River (Va.)—Description
and travel.   4. James River Valley (Va.)—Description
and travel.   I. Theilgard, John.   II. Title.
F232.J2W66   1985   975.5′4   84-24481
ISBN 0-912697-16-4

To Lyn and Laura

CONTENTS

LIST OF ILLUSTRATIONS

In River Time: A Photographic Interpretation
    By John Theilgard

I do not know much about gods; but I think that the river
Is a strong brown god—sullen, untamed and intractable,
Patient to some degree, at first recognized as a frontier;
Useful, untrustworthy, as a conveyor of commerce;
Then only a problem confronting the builder of bridges.
The problem once solved, the brown god is almost forgotten
By the dwellers in cities—ever, however, implacable,
Keeping his seasons and rage, destroyer, reminder
Of what men choose to forget. Unhonored, unpropitiated
By worshippers of the machine, but waiting, watching and
   waiting. . . .
The river is within us. . . .
            "The Dry Salvages," T. S. ELIOT

He who hears the rippling of rivers in these degenerate days will not utterly despair.
            HENRY DAVID THOREAU

IN RIVER TIME

BEGINNINGS

ONE OF the oldest riddles goes something like this: "What keeps running down and out but never stops, and is much older than man is?" The answer—"a river"—looks simple. Still, the riddling continues in one form or another, as people keep finding words to name whatever river they depend on, trying to pin down its fluid realities as they come to see them. So it has been on the James River in Virginia, just as it has been on every other river.

On a map, the James looks much like any other coastal river. Thousands of small streams, often fed by underground mountain springs, repeatedly converge as they move downhill, growing into larger streams sometimes called rivers. Finally each merges into the giant stream, now labeled as the river James, which flows in a general southeasterly direction—sometimes straightaway, sometimes winding. Names have been given to most of the turns in its shifting shape. The river begins at Iron Gate, between the mountains of the Alleghenies, heading southeastward through the Great Valley of Virginia past Buchanan, edging northeast along the base of the Blue Ridge, cutting through

at Glasgow and downhill to Lynchburg, swinging northeast again for forty crooked miles to Scottsville, then
abruptly turning back south, winding to Richmond, dropping through the granite of the Fall Line, and curling seaward, past Hopewell, past Jamestown Island, opening into a
mile-wide flood to Newport News and Hampton Roads,
where it scoops out the base of the Chesapeake Bay. En
route, it turns from fresh to salt water. Then it drops underwater, coursing invisibly until it is finally swallowed by the
Atlantic Ocean at the edge of the continental shelf.

Unlike most great rivers, the James River itself manages
to remain within the confines of a single state, even though
its network stretches over more than 10,000 square miles of
"basin" in three states. It marks many kinds of boundaries,
but it has been spared the troublesome name of state border.
Instead it links the commonwealth of Virginia from its
mountains to the sea, slashing from its northwest peak
almost to the southeast corner.

The James also behaves like every other river. It flows in
one direction, persistently taking the easiest route to the sea.
It gathers and carries the soil and anything else that washes
down with each rain, and then, wherever the current slows,
it deposits its load, shaping banks and islands and raising its
own bed. It can rage with flood when its headwaters are
swollen by rains, or slow to a trickle under dry, blazing
skies. But even in the driest of seasons, it keeps on flowing
from mountain springs that never cease. Always the same
but always changing, sensitive to every mood of weather,
its uplifting bed, and rising sea levels, it shapes itself as it
flows. Like every other river, it seems almost alive.

Beneath its surface, any river is a self-contained world,
for its waters sustain numerous creatures who live by feeding on each other. When that river has both fresh and salt
water, as the James does, it supports many living communities, including some whose life cycles demand a periodic
change of habitat. Fish which prefer cold, deep, or saltier

water may not seek the James, but many other kinds of water-loving animals have come, including human beings. Though they too are occasionally part of the food chain, their dependence is actually on the river's flow—to help provide clean water to make up two-thirds of their body weight.

The story of civilization is closely tied to tales of how these upright, two-legged creatures figured out how to take advantage of the gifts of fresh running water. Archaeologists know that any remaining artifacts or bones of the earliest people will be found along the banks of ancient streams, even though long dry or diverted to other courses, for this is where humans came to drink the water, trap the fish, and harvest wild grains from the floodplains. When they learned to invent ways to harness the water, perhaps lifting it to irrigate or forcing it through mills, then civilization as we know it was under way. So it was on the James, as it had been centuries earlier on the Ganges, the Tigris and Euphrates, the Yangtze, and the Nile. People first came to and up rivers, and there many of their descendents have remained.

The James is a fairly typical stream with few claims to rivery honors. Although its origins are ancient, it is not the oldest river in North America. The New River, its southern sister in the Appalachians, is older, once furnishing the headwaters of the giant Teays which spanned the continent. The James stretches over 335 miles—434 miles if its doubled headwater streams are added, but that is not particularly long for a major river. It cannot compare with the Mississippi in the amount of sediment transported to build new land downstream, though its burden of soil has greatly enriched its floodplains and earned it the affectionate nickname of "old muddy Jeems." It never etched dramatic canyons as the Colorado River did, for its rocky bed is tough and its banks long bore thick forests. Since its basin is water rich, communities have not yet needed to struggle for water rights, and engineers have mostly been able to restrain their damming ways.

As a river, the James is distinctive only because the timing of its floods is so unpredictable; they are liable to come in any season. It is now exceptionally "flashy," able to go from drought to flood level within weeks, creating over time a water level profile with the jagged peaks of an electrocardiogram tracing. Yet this makes the James more rather than less representative a river, for the promise of changes in level and shape is the essence of all rivers. To see this river, then, is to see all rivers to a degree.

Any special distinctions the James bears date from the arrival of people on its banks, especially that of the white man. Perhaps it was an accident that the James was the first river to be permanently settled by enterprising Englishmen, but its history has included a series of other recorded firsts. It has continued to reveal, both early and dramatically, what has happened as Americans approached their wild rivers with love, with hate, but most often with indifference. And its working definition as a river has shifted repeatedly, reflecting the ways it has been seen.

Some people believe that the best way to see a river in its complicated entirety would be to isolate it completely from all human influence. But that would result only in a deep silence since, to be consistent, one would also have to reject the words created to describe the river's processes. Each word necessarily says as much about the perspective and frame of reference of those persons who speak it as it does about the river they seek to characterize. These two realities, subjective and objective, are inseparable. Photographs, too, fall short of depicting the truth of rivers, for they must halt and distort, especially when they try to capture the river's motion. I know of a few persons who understand this, who have become so entranced with the truths spoken by the river that they abandoned both cameras and language to sit beside the river in silence, day after day. There are

The river in flood. — *Richmond Newspapers*

moments when I too find that kind of contemplation of the
river a tempting occupation. But it is a dead end. For better
or worse, the river must be mediated by people. To see the
river whole, one must review that twisting story of how the
river has woven through and shaped the lives of people and,
in turn, been defined and changed by them.

Most of the histories that purport to be about a river,
however, tell instead of events and people, perhaps even of
the houses on its banks and ships on its surface. As for the
river itself, it might just as well have been paved, for they
neither look at its processes and life nor detail the role it has
played as a river in the culture developing on its shores.
Natural histories, on the other hand, focus on the generic
river as a mobile ecosystem or shaper of land and rock, but
the people whose lives it affects are kept at a distance. Recent books which do present the human impact on rivers
tend to become horror stories or soap box sermons, con-
demning those who degrade rivers as well as those who fail
to protect them. These works can also offer worthwhile
perspectives, but none really shows all the dimensions of a
living river surrounded by people.

The story of a river and its people is neither tragic, comic,
nor historical, but contains elements of all three. Its unities
are not exactly those of time or action, even though some of
the actions have had consequences over time. It includes
numerous isolated and sometimes repeated or cyclic events
which do not always fit a historian's neat scheme of cause
and effect. What the events do have in common is setting—
a river which flows continuously though constantly changing shape—where people keep naming and responding to
its processes. The plot complications are all rooted in how
people have and have not seen or tolerated the realities of
their river, and how they have disagreed about them. Char-
acters come and go in this story, each with his or her own
way of seeing and separated in time, but all caught somehow by the magic of the river. In supporting, but not neces-

sarily minor, roles are nonhuman creatures of the river who tend to be victims rather than heroes. The dialogue lies in the words, pictures, or maps which wait in libraries for later generations to read. All in all, a river's story is a strangely structured drama, full of conflicts, revelations, and ironies, that is hard to replay because the script is blotted and sketchy.

Nowhere else, perhaps, is this script more clearly written than it is on the James. Of all the rivers in the world, this is one that educated men approached as a brand-new world and described for those who could not see for themselves. Their eyes were open and their pens poised to record their developing romance with this river. The Spanish who preceded them up the James probably also wrote of their first encounters, but their accounts are still lost in uncatalogued boxes in the Spanish archives. Even if they could be found, they would tell little of the river's subsequent story, since it was the English, not the Spanish, who went on to build their version of a civilized culture there, one which was shaped to a degree by their first impressions and attitudes toward the river. In retrospect, their view of the river may have been even more partial than that of the Indians they displaced; yet what they chose to see has become the heritage of the people of Virginia and even of the United States of America. However, the assumptions they bequeathed have not always served their descendents well.

I did not come to the James as deliberately as those 1607 adventurers did, nor did I expect to find any sort of new world there. In 1971, chance placed me a few miles southwest of the James, near a creek that also crosses the Fall Line. Eventually I started to look closely at the river I crossed twice a day, alerted by the serendipitous meshing of several circumstances in my personal and professional life. I kept finding clues that this river was still a path to relatively unexplored regions—of human geography. Some hints lay in the cadence of foaming rapids, accented by rocks and bird songs, which began to rush through my dream world almost as relentlessly as the river did between its banks. Once, from an airplane, I glimpsed flashing lights leaping out of the darkness, the semaphoric reflections of a new moon skipping over the tidewater islands and sliding down marsh creeks. My attention was completely fastened, though, one warm spring afternoon as I floated through a mist in a canoe, watching raindrop designs collide with the swirling surface, and barely hearing a low but distinct hum beneath the splashing. Like the first explorers, I was finally hooked by the river, and just as determined to mine any gold buried in its physical facts.

At first I thought that going down to the river frequently, mulling over what I was reading in "river-ologies"—geology, hydrology, biology, ecology—would show me its full dimensions. Soon it became clear that any river, especially the James, is much more than its physical facts, more than a "channel of surface drainage water." A river is also what human beings, including myself, have seen and keep seeing it to be. From Henry David Thoreau I had learned much about how natural facts, especially of flowing water, can be named to embody personal/universal ideas, especially if the facts are kept open-ended, unruly and slippery with glimpses of mystery about them. But what he did not teach is that other people's perceptions and experiences with the river, their namings, are also part of its meaning.

Therefore, I turned to other sources, to histories, literature, and other sorts of stories, oral and recorded, to find how people think and feel about "their" river, in this case the James. It has meant trying to recreate not only what they knew, but the contexts of time and more recently, academic discipline, that structure their vision. This style of exploration is not easy, especially when mathematical formulas intrude and historians disagree or relegate the river to footnotes. Treading in alien territory, even if it is intellectual rather than physical, can be discouraging and risky. But the allure of ironies, nuances, and implications buried in even the most precise, technical language has continued to be irresistible. The hidden metaphors are as intriguing as so-called facts, with some of the best insights into how people understand rivers.

Though I am able to move freely through libraries and archives, and, by foot, car, or canoe, along the river, my primary vantage point is naturally where I usually cross the river, over bridges at the Fall Line in Richmond. This too may be a fortunate though uncalculated circumstance. Situated on the river's major barrier to both man and fish, where the tides end and fresh water begins and where more than half of the river's human neighbors have chosen to congregate, I can look both up and down stream. I stand at the very spot where the river has most intensely felt the shaping and mixing hands of man, as well as where those people delegated and elected by Virginians to manage that river reside.

Here too is also one of the few places where the river's depth and rocky bed allow anyone to stand in the middle of the river itself. Although I can literally balance myself here against the river's current, I know that, unaided, I see very little, no matter how clear the water may be. So I keep trying on different lenses, each a fact, an experience, or a perception of the river. Individually each bears unique colors and distortions. The trick has been to mount the lenses together, after eliminating in each as much cloudiness as possible, in hope that eventually much of the subjective astigmatism will be corrected and the colors merged to create a distinctly focused picture. In the process of focusing, somehow the picture that emerges is also a mirror.

It is not just the river I am seeing.

A BIRD'S-EYE VIEW

THE STORY of the river begins in the hieroglyphs of rocks unearthed and translated by geologists. The image they offer is dim and sporadic, covering the 600 million years that this river has known a restless bed, one which has plunged it beneath seas, carved out broad floodplains, and then thrust it into angular new paths. A description of this vast history, then, must be a moving picture, a kind of three-dimensioned holograph which can project through both time and space.

The James officially commences with the marrying of two headwater streams at a place called Iron Gate. Here the cool, placid Cowpasture, receiver of the waters of the Bullpasture and the Calfpasture, meanders through rich farmland, then joins the hot, energetic Jackson, which has been fed by a multitude of warm mineral springs and tumbled down a rocky pass. During the eighteenth century the river carried the name of both a king, James, and a queen, Anne, who insisted that the upper James above the Rivanna be re-named the Fluvanna (or the "river Anna"). Though all these names have been pasted on by man, they seem to acknowledge the reconciling of opposing forces that keep giving birth to the river. But when the unnamed river first emerged, it had to reconcile far fiercer opponents.

The river came to be in a world man would never recognize, one of unbelievable heat and stress and colossal movements, one with little or no vegetation to hold the slopes, only water, wind, and gravity forcing furious erosion. During unimaginable reaches of time, pressed by the weight of miles-deep sediment from the erosion of the bare hills, the earth's crust is believed to have sunk, creating a massive trough filled by a shallow sea which stretched west through what is now named Ohio, south to Alabama, and north through New England, drowning the headwaters of the ancient James.

As the continental plate shifted, the earth continued to flex, compressing and faulting and lifting that sediment more than 250 million years ago into what may have been the highest mountain range on earth. And the waters of the river kept flowing, turning the lofty mountains green and then, bit by bit, transforming them into fertile plains closer to sea level. Again the earth heaved, thrusting up new mountains, again "rejuvenating" its streams by forcing them between steep banks. Still the river kept on flowing, licking at the feet of the shifting hills, cutting its gorges and cascades.

The rock east of the mountains partook of the neighboring upheaval. Heat, movement of the earth, and igneous invasions literally metamorphosed the rock. Like the river above it the rock moved and merged, but in the slowest of tempos. For fifty miles it even detoured the southeasterly river north along insistent faults in the underlying marble, asserting its mastery over the knifing waters.

Though this metamorphic heart of a metamorphic river is called the Piedmont Plain, it is more accurately a plane, repeatedly jutting upwards, repeatedly forcing the river out of its natural aging tendency to wander into wide meanders, giving it instead a sharper, deeper, and more directed second childhood. The piedmont river flows through its wide and ancient floodplain, collecting islands that fish-trapping Indians were to settle and sculpting the metamorphic rock with its red, blue, and yellow mineral streaks.

At the edge of the Piedmont Plain is the Fall Line, a band of granite which formed more than 185 million years ago and now is the base of several cities along the eastern coast of the United States. Here the river drops more than one hundred feet over eight rocky miles, though never suddenly, into the deep sandy sediment beginning below Richmond where three-foot tides still sweep over what were once the shores of prehistoric seas.

Where there is a persistent river, few rocks prove solid enough to withstand it. Even the tough granite at the Fall Line is pocked with holes where smaller, harder, old rocks from upstream have been the tools of tiny whirlpools wearing at fault and joint lines in the rock. During summer droughts, this worn backbone of the East Coast sometimes lies almost fully exposed under the crossing shadows of Richmond's bridges. Such apparent vulnerability is misleading, for here reared a barrier, not just to the first colonists, but to all people who used the watery highway.

Fine tuning that moving holograph again, with a million years converted into minutes, shows the ocean rushing to and even beyond the Fall Line, then ebbing like a great tide, stranding whales in area valleys not once but several times, as recently as 40 million years ago. Add a touch of imagination, and the air at Richmond begins to smell of salt; the roar of the rapids becomes submerged by the boom of the surf. Just beyond the shore might be heard the lumbering of dinosaurs through swamps south of the river, trampling the undergrowth into high quality coal and even a diamond or two.

The ocean has receded now, drowning only a hundred miles of river that persist to the edge of the continental shelf. But the Chesapeake Bay still extends its salty tides to mix with the fresh water over the growing bed of sediment

Iron Gate, near Clifton Forge.—*John Theilgard*

in this Coastal Plain and the part of the river called tidewater. Not subjected to the stress of being rejuvenated by uplifting land, the old river can finally relax here and become sluggish, forming great gaps or bends pierced by impatient floods and men up to the point where large rivers, the Appomattox and the Chickahominy, force the river into line again. The placid appearance and tawny color mask a wealth of life adapted to either fresh or salt water or both, and cover the graveyards of the "royal fish," whales and sturgeon.

Below the Fall Line the river keeps bearing down its slope, forming a tidewater estuary full of marshes and swamps. The James then takes its place as the southernmost of many rivers—the British-named York and the Indian-named Rappahannock, Piankatank, Potomac, Patuxent, Patapsco, Choptank, Susquehanna, and the Sassafras—which mingle their waters in the Bay before they rush through the capes to the ocean.

Somewhere and at some time, a similar estuary where salt and fresh water mix was the birthplace of certain ocean fish who adapted to the fresh water and kept moving upstream. During a drought, these fish found themselves stranded on the margins of swamps and ponds. Eventually the survivors developed primitive lungs, for at that time and place there was far more of the precious oxygen in the air than in the water. In time the kin of those adventurous fish learned to live with the alien element of air and so left the waters of their birth. But they carried the river within them. As Loren Eiseley has written, "As for men, those myriad little detached ponds with their own swarming corpuscular life, what were they but a way that water has of going about beyond the reach of rivers?"

With the coming of man and his self-conscious brain, that river which had flowed cleanly and insistently for eons was no longer to be defined solely by its relationship with the soil and rock. Now it would be defined and thus changed

Passageway through the Blue Ridge at Balcony Falls.
—*Richmond Newspapers*

by the eyes and actions of the children it had once nourished. The river continues to sustain these human beings who settle and roam its banks and play in its water. Though they can chant a litany of practical reasons why they are often drawn to the river, perhaps none is as strong as the deep compulsion to return home, to touch base once again. Perhaps like me, they see in the river images of entropy and renewal, and above all, themselves. They too may want to know not only the river, but the life that is the river that flows through us all.

PRIMITIVE LEGACIES

THE RIVER which early people first encountered, probably over ten thousand years ago at the end of the last ice age, looked quite different from the river of today. From the mountains to the sea it was a braided stream, broken up and meandering restlessly back and forth along broad gravelly strips of land which were grazed by giant herbivores. There was no Chesapeake Bay in those days before the sea level rose with the melting of glacial ice, only the great Susquehanna River bearing south to join the James in carrying fresh water over the exposed continental shelf. There were also no fish leaving the ocean en masse each spring to spawn in the fresh waters of the James. These first people, called Paleo–Indians, saw no particular advantage to settling along rivers since there were few fish to eat. Usually they stayed in small groups, moving restlessly through the forests of northern spruce and pine, hunting mammoths and mastodons.

The climate continued to warm. As the snow caps melted on the mountains, the James carried vast loads of eroded silt in the rising waters which were cutting down into its present bed. The wide floodplains became more fertile, the forests changed, and more Indians came to hunt, fish, and gather food, especially around the mouth of the river.

Several millennia ago, the Chesapeake Bay began forming as the rising seas invaded and drowned the Susquehanna and the lowest reaches of the James. As the Bay became saltier, anadromous or freshwater spawning fish such as shad, herring, and the giant sturgeon began ascending the James, perhaps four thousand years ago. Indians whom anthropologists have labeled the Savannah River people also came to the river's mouth and eventually moved upstream, following the fish, sometimes settling on the same sites chosen by other tribes centuries before. They understood well that "April is the cruellest month." The blooming of spring life ironically coincided with their starving times, for in spring the game was hidden by the new growth, the nuts were rotten, and harvest of berries and wild grain was months away. For them the river—with its dependable fish runs from March through June and the wild grains sprouting on the floodplains—promised survival, no less. It determined where, how, and even whether they could live.

In that wilderness the river was the only road, and virtually every Indian village was located on a river or a large creek. Rough canoes, burned and scraped out of virgin timber, made the exchange of goods possible, sometimes over remarkably long distances. The water level was lower then, as was the level of the sea, but the James could still be an unpredictable river, often reduced by drought or swollen by flood, and its swift currents ran in only one direction. Perhaps the advantages of the linkage it provided were offset by the necessity for the groups to spread out, for even the fertile floodplains in the piedmont region could not support large numbers of people after the fish returned to the sea.

In some ways the river was a kind of natural Berlin Wall which raised social and cultural barriers. Not surprisingly, tribes tended to ally more with groups on their side of the river. But the greatest demarcation was at the Fall Line, the buffer zone that the Powhatan Indians named Paquachowng.

Above the Falls in the Piedmont Plain were the Monacans, people of Siouian linguistic origins who were settled in small groups along the river's floodplain. They were family centered and rarely roamed far for their food, a "sedentary" people (as anthropologists say) who preferred to catch the fish and gather grain which grew from seeds first swept downstream from the fertile hills. They stripped and felled trees on the islands and banks to encourage the seeds which were gifts of the floods. Probably they did not actually plant crops of maize, beans, and squash until about 1000 A.D.

Archaeologists now believe that these piedmont people lived in what has been termed a segmentary confederacy. The small bands stayed to themselves except for the necessary marriages and battles against common enemies, especially the aggressive Iroquois who kept raiding from the west. By stretching along the river, they were quite literally segmented in organization. There may have even been substantial language barriers between the tribes on the James and those on the piedmont portion of the Rappahannock River to the north. There was little political organization of the basically egalitarian Monacans, although there was a "central place" at Rassawek, on the broad alluvial land between the James and the Rivanna rivers.

The Monacans tended their own gardens beside the great fresh water stream, occasionally challenging the territorial boundaries of tribes below the Falls, though probably more to trade their soapstone pottery than to gain food. Ordinarily they stayed well above the buffer zone of the Fall Line where the Powhatan Indians sometimes hunted.

The Indians in the tidewater river, of Algonquin origin, were more numerous and closer neighbors, but they were less settled. With little fertile floodplain available, since that land had been drowned by the rising river waters, these Indians supplemented farming by hunting deer, bear, and squirrel, fishing, and gathering nuts and berries whenever and wherever they could be found. The life of the Coastal Plain was highly diverse, with an abundance of different food sources varying by season. Thus these tribes, which the English identified as the Powhatans, stayed relatively mobile, moving from river to uplands to swamps with their wigwams, following their food and camping near fresh springs.

The wide river below the Fall Line, which branched into many streams and marshes, offered easy access and communication for a people who had learned early how to turn trees into dugout canoes. This access, plus the need to co-ordinate food-gathering activities, evidently encouraged a more sophisticated tribal organization than the Monacans knew. Eventually more than thirty tribes joined in what by 1607 was called the Powhatan Confederacy, a loose hierar-chical political organization managed by the chief or wero-wance, the wily Powhatan, assisted by Opechancanough. Chiefdoms were usually hereditary, passing through broth-ers, then sisters, then the sisters' sons. Though allied, each tribe roamed a clearly delineated territory.

Less is known about how the other major barrier on the river, the Blue Ridge mountain range, affected Indian cul-ture. Here the river, without extensive fertile plains or the spring fish runs, may well have played only a slight role in the lives of the Iroquois who hunted in the mountains and roved in small bands through the valleys of the James and the Shenandoah.

Although the James is one river, its divided nature, then, spawned at least two cultures, with surprisingly diverse structures. By adapting to the different conditions and rhythms of the river, each developed in turn rather different styles of living. The river was the prime shaper of their daily lives.

What we know about the Paleo-Indians or the Monacans

Indians at work on a dugout canoe, from Thomas Hariot's *A Brief and True Report.* — *Virginia State Library*

and the Powhatans before the year 1607 either has been deduced from the projectile points and shards of a few archaeological digs or was reported by the early colonists, especially John Smith. Neither source gives much basis for understanding the Indians' deepest emotions about the river. These we must surmise.

The first human beings to come to this river were probably slow to gain any sense of mastery over the river, and far slower to understand that any control of these relentlessly flowing waters was possible or desirable. So intimately dependent on the river were they for its sweet waters, its fish, its attractions for game, its protection, even for a sense of location and direction, that they accepted it as a major fact of their natural existence. They took its gifts as they could, very likely unable to imagine that there could be more. The rhythms of their lives were governed by those of nature, as were those of the animals they hunted.

At some point in the dim prehistoric past, these peoples became aware of themselves as being somehow separate from nature. It was then that they began seeing and questioning the river. How were they to explain its power? Its constant changes and yet its perpetual flow? What if it should stop or go away? How could mere people placate the anger of its flooding waters and lure the fish into reach?

We have no way of knowing how or when these particular people answered these and other questions about their river. We do, however, have some idea of answers from other primitive peoples, for the clues still lie at the base of myths and religions. The river, like the skies, the forests, or the mountains, has long been the home of powerful and inexplicable gods and a symbol almost too deep for words for understanding birth, death, and life's renewal.

The ancient gods of the rivers were rarely named or described, for like the river they were shapeshifters and sometimes even androgynous, as the Greek myths tell us. Some also had the power to transform intruders into fish-men or fountains. Each river or spring had its own god or nymph which guarded it and embodied the sacredness of flowing waters. Nymphs who were given names could be nurturing, for they sometimes raised children to be heroes, or they could be destructive, visiting madness on any man who spied them at midday.

These watery gods commanded respect, veneration, and even sacrifice, though not love nor strong roles in the mythic tales. They were essentially unformed and metamorphic, often nameless, more in the realm of the potential than the fully realized, even in the farthest stretches of men's imaginations. Rarely did they interfere in the affairs of men directly, for their link with primordial creation put them generally beyond time and history. Yet when men sought wisdom and foresight, it was often to the springs and fresh waters that they came to consult with the resident maiden oracle, as at Delphi in Greece. It is no coincidence that the finding of fresh water has long been called divining.

The river has been worshipped primarily as the bringer of life, as germinative, containing the potential for all forms of life. And so it was, in ways we are just now beginning to comprehend. The Indians on the James seem to have venerated the river's fertility. They learned that the river brought seeds in its flooding waters, for their ax-heads still clutter islands of the piedmont James where the Monacans once cleared trees to make certain that the seeds flourished. Since they grew their crops on the floodplain, they evidently understood that the silt deposited by the river, past and present, bore the most abundant and fruitful vegetation.

But there is no way the Indians or other primitive peoples could have consciously known that all animals breathing the oxygen of the air had their origin in the fresh waters, nor that the ages and ages of rains and erosion on the hard earth long before man appeared, as the waters ran to the sea, had turned rock into soil fit for life. Yet for almost every primitive culture situated on a fertile river, whether on the Ganges or between the Tigris and Euphrates, the recurring myths of creation show life emerging from a primeval watery chaos. So it may have been for the Indians on the James, explaining why they often placed fish on their hills of corn seed.

Whether these Indians ever felt compelled to make drastic sacrifices to guarantee the fertile powers of the water is unknown. It is improbable, though, for this is a relatively dependable river, which never dries up. Nevertheless, this river is unpredictable. There were surely fluctuations in the fish runs, as well as floods which came too late and so submerged, not planted, the rough fields.

The early colonists, for all their meticulous description of the curious dress and social habits of the "savages," were a bit derelict in recording the rituals of the Indians. What they did notice, they usually could not understand. But a time-honored rite of purification and sacrifice to the river is suggested by the account of William White, who lived with the Powhatan Indians during the summer of 1607.

As Richard Hakluyt recorded White's story:

the morning by break of day, before they eate or drinke both men, women and children, that be above tenne yeeres of age runnes into the water, there washes themselves a good while till the Sunne riseth, then offer Sacrifice to it, strewing Tobacco on Water or Land, honouring the Sunne as their God, likewise they doe it at the setting of the Sunne.

What the English interpreted as simple sun worship and unnecessary bathing appears to include reverential recognition of the cleansing powers of the flowing river.

The ceremonial sacrifice of tobacco, prized by the Indians as a source of pleasure as well as a religious symbol, especially after a storm, also astonished the colonists. Robert Beverley assumed almost a century later that such rituals were intended to pacify or conquer the river. He noted that "when they cross any great Water, or violent Fresh, or Torrent they throw Tobacco, Puccoon, Peak . . . to intreat the Spirit residing there, to grant them a safe passage." The colonists' explanations may well show more about their perspective on the river as a force to be tamed than about the Indian worship of the river's powers. Evidently many of the Indians' religious rituals centered on the river. But the kind of spiritual wealth the sacrificial tobacco represented had little meaning to the representatives of the London Company.

Water also played a key role in Indian medical practices. The roots and bark ingested for various ailments were ground and infused in water. If external application seemed more appropriate, water was used to make a poultice. But the flow of the river was imitated most in the Indians' frequent use of sweating huts, actually saunas in the Finnish style, followed by a plunge into cold water to carry off "all the Crudities contracted in their Bodies," as Beverley put it. Not incidentally perhaps, the Indians were consistently described as very healthy people before the white man's diseases began wasting them, an observation borne out by the archaeological record of their bones.

The river must have also given the Indians a peaceful sense of continuity, for it was the unending witness of past and future generations. Trees could rot and hills could be diminished by erosion, but the river kept on flowing. Though, like life, the river runs in only one direction, somehow it is mysteriously and constantly renewed. Surely here the Indians found both hope for immortality and verification of the single direction of time, the bearer of loss and death.

A myth now popular has it that American Indians worshipped nature and its indwelling spirits from arm's length, and that fear or reverence made them reluctant to tap nature's bounty. Perhaps this notion has been fostered by those who have struggled to preserve the more pristine wilderness areas where men left few if any marks. But even those Englishmen who thought they had discovered virgin land, a kind of untilled, primeval garden of Eden which lay awaiting their god-sent cultivation and redemption, had to admit that the Indians knew well how to use nature's gifts to fill their needs.

The accounts sent back to England are filled with details about how the Indians farmed, fished, and hunted. But, oddly enough, admiration for the effectiveness and ingenuity of these practices did not become emulation. As John Smith wrote in the fall of 1608, "Though there be fish in the Sea, foules in the ayre, and Beasts in the woodes, their bounds are so large, they so wilde, and we so weake and ignorant, we cannot much trouble them." The Indians had no such problems. In turn, the English, like other European newcomers, had no compunctions about trading copper trinkets for bushels of corn and taking full advantage of Indian generosity at harvest time. But as representatives of a superior Christian civilization, they felt that they must resist the temptation to learn from savages.

The English had particular trouble understanding the Indian concept of property ownership. Although tribes had territorial boundaries, the idea of exclusive possession of the land was alien to them. The land and the river belonged only to the people who used them, when they used them, and to the generations yet unborn. They did not even leave their river a single name. It was given many names in the typical Indian fashion, names associated with parts of the river that invited description (like the Falls) or, more often, with tribes whose activities bounded a particular segment for a while. For the Indians, a river and its people were connected by naming.

The Indians felt free to take from nature what they needed to survive, but they took little more, and shared any excesses from good harvests with less fortunate neighbors, even hungry white men. Perhaps they felt that to use the gifts of the earth too liberally, beyond what could be replaced naturally, could waste what they and their children's children would later need. Thus, though the river had known Indians fishing its waters and settling on its banks and islands for thousands of years, the water remained sweet and fertile. They were effective fishermen, but they recognized certain limits. They left few signs of their long tenure: two distinct kinds of arrowheads, some Monacan pots of soapstone, a few stone fish weirs at shallow rocky places, and possibly some sediment in the bed eroded from the lands cleared above the Falls for farming. Nothing, though, really disturbed the river or its life.

It would be a mistake to romanticize the Indians' treatment of nature, forgetting that they were relatively few in number and widely scattered (probably there were never more than a few thousand in Virginia at most). They lacked tools to change their environment seriously, even if they had wanted to. The Monacans in particular used fire freely to clear trees from the floodplain, and the only reason more soil did not wash into the river was that they saw no reason to remove stumps or work over their fields. The effects of subsistence living by a relatively small number of people could be easily absorbed and repaired, if necessary, by natural processes.

But even granting these facts, we must acknowledge that the Indians could literally see and adapt to the river's processes far better than the white conquerers were willing to do, even though they actually knew less "science." Their reluctance to take more from nature than they needed, possibly from fear that nature might not continue to provide so generously, and their respect for the river's moods were attitudes alien to the people who were to displace them. We cannot know for certain how the river would have fared under continued Indian stewardship, especially if the population had grown, but it is fair to assume that the river's subsequent history could have been different.

There is at least one place on the river where it is possible today to look back through time, to glimpse the continuity the Indians must have felt. About two miles up Powell

Creek, south of Hopewell in the tidewater estuary, is land high between two marshes which several groups of Indians, especially the Algonquin tribe called the Weyanoke or Wea-noc, found to be choice living ground for as long as nine or ten thousand years. In 1607 John Smith counted 340 people here and in four other Weyanoke villages on both sides of the river. This location furnished fertile soil replenished from higher ground, abundant fresh water from springs and the creek, wildlife which came to drink and live on the quiet marshy creek, and protection from invasion by men or floods. Neither eroded nor mined for gravel, the soil over the bones and treasures of this culture remained untouched for centuries. For the past six years, an independent group of archaeologists has been digging at this spot, piecing together the kind of life and death acted out on these banks.

There are not many places I would consider hallowed ground, but this remote site would head my list. I had taken barely ten steps before I found a shard of pottery over two thousand years old with a surprisingly sophisticated fabric design pressed into the river clay. A little digging revealed many more such shards along with stone chips discarded from centuries of projectile point making. These fragments lying in the fill from earlier digging may not have been special enough for the archaeologists to keep after recording their precise position, shape, and condition, but they made the ground literally come alive for me. Under glass was the systematic proof of these early people's growing mastery in shaping the stones and shells from beside the river. Each object had its niche in the long history that the chief archaeologist sketched for me as he chipped at a stone, making it an arrowhead the Indians would have acknowledged as well crafted.

As we dug that afternoon, learning how to name what we unearthed, we uncovered a midden, a kitchen pit topped by deer bones with human teeth marks still on them. Speculating on what might lie beneath those bones interested me more than actually finding objects to measure or photograph, but then I am not a scientist. As we sifted through the rich black dirt, I realized that even in a few hours my eyes were beginning to refocus, to see new dimensions around me. Roots and oyster shells were easy to discard, but almost nothing else was tossed aside as we carefully felt for evidence of the ancient folk who now seemed so close.

Even the creek seemed different after we finished digging, now teeming with waterfowl and fish I had not noticed before. We would find there none of the evidence of the Indians' lives, though it was the water which had repeatedly drawn different groups of Indians to this spot. I knew that I too would have to come back, perhaps to help stand guard some warm night and to dream myself into the spirits of these people my ancestors had once forced away from the river.

Dig as we may, there is still much we can only guess about the meaning this river may have held for the simple folk on its shores. Was the river considered a nourishing mother, a vengeful father, or both, like the androgynous god of the Nile? Were its waters reputed to heal or to restore youth? Were its fish sacred? Did the Indian myths of death speak of a journey across the river? Was the pollution of the stream from which they drank forbidden, as it was in India and Babylon? We can only guess. But we can be certain that the river was vital to their emotional and spiritual as well as their physical lives. What the Weyanoke dig teaches is that the Indians recognized and responded to the river's living mastery for centuries, long before the white man came with his civilizing guns, concepts of profit and ownership, and faith that nature could provide liberally and infinitely.

CONQUERORS AND
CIVILIZERS

IT WAS no accident that the English settlers, like all European explorers, quickly named the river they had discovered as a first step in establishing their claim. From the beginning they were determined to leave their mark on a nature that they saw as a hostile wilderness. As representatives of an advanced civilization, they felt it their duty to subdue the earth. Certainly they could praise the river for its fertile banks and fish and even appreciate its beauty, but unlike the Indians they viewed it as a road to wealth. One of the first reports that Captain Newport carried back to England was appropriately titled "The Discription of the now discovered River and Country of Virginia; with the Liklyhood of ensuing ritches, by Englands ayd and industry." The battle lines separating the white man and his European notions about ownership and civilization from nature and its resident red man were already drawn. For years the outcome was in doubt, although the Indians were clearly at a disadvantage in fighting for a river they thought no man or group of men could own.

The drama which unfolded as these two cultures clashed
was to be reenacted continually along each river which they
both prized. At the root of the conflict were two opposing
ways of seeing the river. Its resolution would set the pattern
for how the river would be treated by its human neighbors
for centuries to come. At first, the English could not praise
the river enough, though they did not know much about it.
But as their mythic expectations gave way to the reality of
living with that river, it was relegated to the scenic background of their histories. They soon ceased to describe the
river except as a convenient highway, though sometimes
they viewed it as being as unmanageable as the Indians
had been.

The James may have been a new river to them, but the
English view of rivers had already been conditioned by another river an ocean away. Most knew the Thames, a tidal
river then edged by an overcrowded city of half a million
people. Like urbanites since that time, Londoners thought
little more of the river than they would of any other highway that was troublesome to cross. They hardly realized
that the same tides which gave a handy push to boat traffic
also kept the river water relatively turgid and sluggish at
London, so that whatever went into the river—and everything did—stayed for a while. With each rainstorm the sewage, dumped unceremoniously into ditches and the streets,
was transported down to the river. Many people of London
drank of the river's waters, especially those who could not
afford beer, and many paid the price of typhoid fever, chol-
era, hepatitis, and dysentery. They knew that life was short,
but not why.

Some of the people who came to the James were pos-
sessed by a dream of far more wondrous rivers than the
Thames. This dream had been liberally fed by accounts of
the voyages of Jacques Cartier to the St. Lawrence, John
Hariot and Ralph Lane to the Roanoke and Chowan, and
James Rosier to the St. George's. Many of these were pub-

lished by Richard Hakluyt, a geographer much enamoured
of golden, westward-leading rivers. These popular works,
often dispensing with inconvenient facts, lauded the glorious
waterways which penetrated the continent of the new world
to lead bold dreamers to the untold wealth of the Indies
which was surely to be found a few more days upstream.
Undeterred by the disappearance of the colonists placed on
Roanoke Island in North Carolina's Albemarle Sound by Sir
Walter Raleigh, a group of Londoners, primarily merchants,
formed a joint-stock company to finance a colonizing expedition to the probable northwest passage, or failing to find
that, to the raw materials which lay waiting transformation
into profit.

The London Council's "Instructions given by way of Advice," written by Hakluyt and given to the group of 104 or
105 prospective colonists (accounts vary) who gathered
in December of 1606 to embark on three tiny ships for
Virginia, show the English obsession with the fabled rivers.
They were told to:

Do your best Endeavour to find out a Safe port in the Entrance of
Some navigable River making Choise of Such a one as runneth fur-
thest into the Land, And if you happen to Discover Divers portable
Rivers and amongst them any one that hath two main branches if the
Difference be not Great make Choise of that which bendeth most
towards the Northwest for that way shall You soonest find the
Other Sea.

Their first task, even before landing "Victual and munitions," was to "Let Captain Newport Discover how far that
River may be found navigable that you may make Election
of the Strongest, most Fertile and wholesome place." The
armchair travelers specifically recommended "A place you
may perchance find a hundred miles from the Rivers mouth
and the farther up the better" so that enemies may be beat
"from both sides of your River where it is Narrowest."
After landing, forty men were to spend "two Months in

32

Discovery of the River above," disembarking with pickaxes to look for minerals.

Hakluyt left no question about the main goal of this river expedition:

You must Observe if you can Whether the River on which you Plant Doth Spring out of Mountains or out of Lakes. If it be out of any Lake the passage to the Other Sea will be the more Easy & it is Like Enough that Out of the same Lake you shall find Some Spring which run the Contrary way toward the East India Sea.

It was to be years before the myth of the "Other Sea" beyond the Appalachians gave way to reality; as late as 1650, the sea appeared on a British map. For the first colonists, though, the dream of South Sea wealth colored their perspective of the river, keeping them from seeing more mundane realities.

On December 20, 1606, three ships under the command of Captain Newport, the *Susan Constant*, the *Godspeed*, and the *Discovery*, set sail on the Thames for Virginia. But the English river was not ready to let them go right away. Adverse sea winds and rough water stranded the ships at the Downs near where the river empties into the sea. The Reverend Hunt almost died of typhoid fever as they lay becalmed, but he refused to give up his holy mission to the savages and return to his nearby home. As the long weeks passed, the men aboard grew at least as contentious as the winds. Finally in February, the weather changed and the frustrated and quarreling men with short provisions set out for the new world.

The English were not the first white men to sail into the Chesapeake Bay. The Spanish had sent Jesuit missionaries in 1570, following up a 1560 expedition, but they were soon wiped out by Indians. Another aborted settlement attempt originated from Raleigh's colony on Roanoke Island in 1585. In 1588, the Spanish Captain Vicente Gonzalez went up as far as the Potomac, very likely looking for survivors of the

Reproductions of the *Susan Constant*, *Godspeed* and *Discovery*, at Jamestown Landing. — *Virginia Division of Tourism*

Jesuit mission. The first Englishman to sail these waters came in 1603, but Bartholomew Gilbert paid for his adventure with his life at the hands of Indians.

Some historians even report a Spanish settlement attempt on the river itself, near what would become Jamestown Island, at the unbelievably early date of 1526. Lucas Vasquez d'Ayllon is said to have brought 600 men and women, including many Negro slaves, 100 horses, and a Jesuit named Antonio Montesino to build a town named San Miguel. But d'Ayllon died of fever and the settlers suffered "hunger and sickness, internecine quarrels, negro insurrection, and attacks from the Indians"; the survivors were shipwrecked en route to Spain. As fate would have it, the scenario 81 years later would not be too different, except that more ships kept coming.

The men sent by the London Company were either ignorant of this dismal history or uncommonly brave, greedy, or desperate, or all of the above. They were not mistaken in their expectation of Indian hostility. Nevertheless, they were so eager to touch land that a party went ashore after the ships first anchored just west of Cape Henry. After sunset, they were attacked by "Savages creeping upon all foures, from the Hills, like Beares, with their Bowes in their mouthes" and two white men were injured, as George Percy's journal observations tell us. From that time, the English constantly "suspictioned villainie."

The fleet soon turned into the river, searching for the spot which best fit the instructions they carried. If they felt that their progress was being watched by an Indian behind every tree, they were not too far wrong. A number of Indian warriors had come to the river from miles around after hearing of the first landing, curious to see these strange boats and pale men, but with their bows and arrows ready. They too waited to see where the ships would land.

The place which seemed to fit Hakluyt's instructions best was a low-lying peninsula, about two miles long and one mile wide over thirty miles upstream, which was linked to the mainland by a narrow sand bar. Beside it was a deep river channel carved by erosion (which would continue to gnaw at the island). On the other side was the Back River, actually a deep marsh creek which could shelter ships. Though the English were delighted to have found a place of easy anchor and defense, there were many other conditions they failed to consider. The fact that there were no Indians residing on the land that May morning should have been a clue.

This island, which the settlers promptly named for their king, was probably the worst piece of real estate on the river in the summer time, and the Indians knew it. It lay very low, invaded by stagnant swamps, and it had no freshwater springs. Salt water mixed with fresh water in the summer at that point of the river to create what is now called a "zone of maximum turbidity." This meant that the river was often turgid and brackish at low water, not at all suitable for drinking. Perhaps the English were reminded of the tidal Thames at London, and thus saw no problem. Defense and navigation, not the quality of the water they had no intention of drinking, were the prime considerations.

It is not difficult to understand why the Indians, poised for attack, put away their weapons and generally left the white men alone. We have their own words for the reason. George Percy reported that some of the Indians in the villages the English visited on their first trip to the Falls became upset at "our planting in the Countrie." Their leader reassured them, "very wisely of a Savage," saying, "Why should you bee offended with them as long as they hurt you not, nor take any thing away by force. They take but a little waste ground which doth you nor any of us any good." That waste ground which the Indians conceded, especially after the nearby Paspahegh Indians had been given some copper, became Jamestown.

The English had no idea that their island location was

dangerous. After all, they had been thoroughly prepared to find a majestic river, and that is exactly what they saw. Percy asserted that "This River which wee have discovered is one of the famousest Rivers that ever was found by any Christian." This river and its banks were perceived as being a type of paradise, for Percy spoke of its "goodliest Woods" and "Vines in great abundance, which hang in great clusters on many Trees," just waiting harvest by eager hands. Even the ground was "bespred with many sweet and delicate flowres of divers colours and kindes" and the fruit of "Strawberries, Mulberries, Rasberries, and Fruites unknowne." The river itself was bursting with abundance with its many branches "which runne flowing through the Woods with great plentie of fish of all kindes; as for Sturgeon, all the World cannot be compared to it." No wonder people thought that here was a land and river which would provide without much work on their part, and they kept streaming into ships, disregarding rumors of starvation and disease.

A similar ecstatic response to the river is found in a letter written in June, probably by Edward Maria Wingfield: "Wee are sett down 80 miles within a River, for breadth, sweetnes of water, length navigable upp into the contry deepe and bold Channell so stored with Sturgion and other sweete Fish as no mans fortune hath ever possessed the like." Assured that they had found the ultimate river, he concluded that "wee think if more maie be wishe'd in a River it wilbe founde." The myth of the wondrous river had survived the reality of its discovery.

Like the gold at the end of a rainbow river, the lure of the South Sea still beckoned. Newport, Smith, and twenty men took the shallop they had built up the river in late May, quizzing the Indians along the way about the shape and headwaters of the river. One Indian obligingly drew a map showing waterfalls, boundaries of two strong (enemy) nations, mountains, and, a week's or ten days' journey away, a great body of water. Upon inquiry, several Indians "recalled" that the great sea was salt, for they were anxious to please these visitors bearing gifts who asked such strange questions.

The barrier of the Falls proved insurmountable, especially since the Indians refused to guide the English through the enemy territory. A frustrated Captain Smith failed to see much beauty in these "great craggy stones in the midst of the river, where the water falleth so rudely, and with such a violence, as not any boat can possibly pass." Another report, probably written by Gabriel Archer, projected mercantile possibilities in this area of "overfall, where the water falls downe from huge great Rockes: making in the fall five or six several Ilettes, very fitt for the buylding of water milnes thereon." Archer was so certain of the sea beyond the mountains that he felt no need to provide details for his English readers: "beyond this the Falls not two dayes journey, it the river hath two branches which come through a high stoney Country from certaine huge mountains called Quirank, beyond which needs no relacion."

Before leaving the Falls on this first expedition, the English "set up a Crosse at the head of this River, naming it Kings River, where we proclaimed James King of England to have the most right unto it," as Percy wrote. To name this river was to claim it for England. The Indians settled below the Falls under Powhatan's rule were justifiably puzzled and disturbed by this rite of rights, but Newport smoothly explained that the two sticks bound together represented the two kings, Indian and English, and the name Kings River commemorated their union.

How could the English have so arrogantly established their ownership of the Indian river? The answer lies deep in attitudes toward nature and its resident Indians formed long before 1607, as well as the race with Spain to claim the new world. The fact that the Indian had left little evidence of his occupation of the land, that even in farming he made hills instead of extensively turning the earth, was prima facie evidence that he had not dominated nature and thus did not truly own the land. Besides, the Indians were savages in need of the civilizing order of Christianity. As Bernard Sheehan argues, it made little difference whether they were noble primitives or the devil's servants; either way they were uncivilized animals, not yet deserving of full human status. This reasoning might not have held as well had the Indians first encountered by the English been the apparently more settled and agricultural Monacans. Yet some other excuse would have been found, for the English intended to possess the river and its lands by fair means or foul.

Captain Newport soon left for England, "leaving us (one hundred and foure persons) verie bare and scantie of victualls, furthermore in warres and in danger of savages," as Smith complained. There was no more beer to drink, only river water. Unwilling and unable to find food as the Indians did or settle for a diet different from the accustomed one, the men began to die from a combination of starvation and disease. By the end of the summer of 1607, only 35 to 40 men still lived.

Each summer for the next several years the gruesome tale was to be the same. Many out of each new group of colonists succumbed in the summer before they had been properly "seasoned." George Percy, so quick to see the river's beauty, also recognized the river's role in the mortality rate. As he explained, "our food was but a small Can of Barlie sod in water, to five men a day, our drinke cold water taken out of the River, which was at a floud verie salt, at a low tide full of slime and filth, which was the destruction of many of our men." This is an apt description of America's first major public health crisis.

At least one historian, Carville Earle, who has compared the reported medical symptoms with the composition of the river during summer droughts, when the wedge of salt water generally moves up to the Jamestown area of the river, agrees with Percy's assessment. With relatively little movement of the water caused by the mixture of salt and fresh water, sewage which washed into the river stayed to spread typhoid fever and dysentery, as it did in the Thames. There were likely several carriers of those London-bred bacteria; ironically, one may have been the Reverend Hunt, who patiently tended and cooked for the sick. The high salt content of water taken when the tide was rising also may have literally poisoned the men, making them too lethargic even to dig a well for fresh water. Those that were eventually dug were shallow and probably contaminated, like the river.

I can visualize the Indians camped at the fresh springs on high ground, nodding their heads wisely at rumors of the deaths of the English and restraining eager young warriors, counseling patience while these white strangers died off. But the ships kept on coming, filled with new settlers, and the people kept on dying. Soon malaria, spread by marsh-bred mosquitoes which had fed on infected European blood, also began taking a heavy toll. By 1624, of the 5,000 who had come to Virginia (not counting infants born after arrival), only about 1,000 remained according to conservative estimates. Some historians say that as many as six colonists died for every one that survived. These figures include the nearly 350 settlers killed in the 1622 massacre, when the Indians finally lost patience, for the ships and men never seemed to stop coming. At least half of the earliest colonists died of water-related diseases at Jamestown. The English assumed that the river would sustain them, without any effort on their part to know it as intimately at the Indians had. Perhaps they were blinded by their own myth of a golden river created solely to serve their needs and lust for wealth.

CHAMPIONS OF THE
GOLDEN RIVER

AT MY Powell Creek perch, I sift through black dirt filled with Renaissance-styled buttons and pieces of metal mingled with arrowheads and bits of bone. These remind me that for decades the question of ownership of the river land was very much contested. Both Indians and English repeatedly claimed this soil, though not at the same time, for there was no allowance for sharing.

Either here or very close by on the river is the place where the soldier John Smith first met Opechancanough as he returned from the Fall Line, where he and Captain Newport had just named the river. Smith hardly noticed this imposing chief of the Pamunkey tribe, being far more absorbed by reports of a salt sea upstream and premonition of trouble downstream. Rather than tarrying to converse with the chief so richly decorated with pearls and copper, he rushed to Jamestown, arriving just in time to thwart a sneak Indian attack. He was a man spoiling for a good fight, but he never suspected that he had just met the young colony's most formidable human opponent, the instigator of many such attacks.

The buried treasures of the archaeologist are eloquent, but they speak too softly for me. It is time to look at the river through the eyes of John Smith, the James' first chronicler and prime mapmaker. Although he lived in Virginia for only two years and a summer, this feisty little redheaded man who thrived on adventure and exaggeration would become a prototype of the American hero. Likewise, his pragmatic perspective of the river and its people helped shape attitudes which persist.

The battle between two cultures, one "civilized" and the other "savage," for possession of the rivers and their fertile lands, could not have offered less likely champions for each side. The English reluctantly fielded the ambitious commoner, John Smith; the Indians looked to Opechancanough, a prince of "large Stature, noble Presence, and extraordinary parts." Although they never formally met on a battleground, much to Smith's regret, the conflict between these larger-than-life heroes focuses the greater one between their people.

Though Smith was one of the youngest men to embark for Virginia in 1606, he was also the only one qualified by his experiences with alien and hostile cultures to deal effectively with the Indians. By his own account, he was already a man of the world, though of common English birth, who had been a mercenary soldier of fortune throughout Europe and a student of Marcus Aurelius and Machiavelli. The highlight of his military career was the beheading of three Turks who had challenged him to separate duels of mortal combat at the dawn of three days. Thus Smith won time for the Transylvanian troops he had joined to gather and consequently win. He was rewarded by his commander, King Zsigmond, with promises of gold and a shield bearing three heads to which someone (Smith?) added the motto, *Vincere est vivere* (To Conquer is to Live). Thus Smith could legi-

C. Smith taketh the King of Pamavnkee prisoner 1608

Captain John Smith threatens Opechancanough, from Smith's *Generall Historie.*—*Virginia State Library*

timately consider himself a gentleman, as he desperately wanted. That is, if anyone would believe him. He moved on to other adventures in Turkey and Russia, as soldier and slave, becoming a man who would rely on his wits, nerve, and linguistic skills to wriggle out of tight spots. It is no wonder that, when Smith returned home at the age of twenty-four, he joined the efforts to launch the expedition to Virginia, aided by old friends, the wealthy and aristocratic Berties. Here finally would be a chance to prove his valor to English eyes.

The story sounds so fantastic, like an updated Odysseus living by his wit and a large reserve of luck, that scholars for years labeled Smith a liar and no gentleman at all. Even his contemporaries suspected him of going beyond the boundaries of acceptable Renaissance braggadocio. But evidence has been painstakingly unearthed that corroborates the gist of Smith's tale. Like the rivers of Virginia that he "discovered," myth and fact have become mixed to the point that truth becomes a chimera not worth pinning down.

The background of his opponent is even more mysterious and debatable. Although Smith called him the (half?) brother of Powhatan, Opechancanough, whose name translates as "He Whose Soul is White," seems to have had more exotic origins. His experiences in other lands may have almost matched Smith's. Robert Beverley reports that the Indians called him "a Prince of a Foreign Nation" who came to the Algonquin Indians "a great way from the South-West." He speculated that Opechancanough might have come from the "Spanish Indians, some-where near Mexico." There is more to this tale than an English assumption that a smart Indian must have had extended contact with another civilization.

Evidently there was a Virginian Indian, named Don Luis de Velasco by the Spaniards but said to be related to Powhatan (as father or elder brother?), who joined or was abducted by a Spanish expedition in the Chesapeake Bay around 1560. After traveling to Spain, then the Caribbean and Mexico, in futile attempts to return home, he finally arrived on the James with a group of Jesuit missionaries in 1570. He rather promptly rejected his Christian conversion, taking several wives, and soon murdered the Jesuits. Was he Opechancanough? Or was Don Luis actually Powhatan's father, who brought his Indian servant from Mexico (Opechancanough) and recognized him as a foster son? There are several possibilities. Tradition has it that Opechancanough, whoever he was, named little Pocahontas "Matoaka," a name thought to be of Aztec and not Algonquin origin. Had he written his own history, it would likely have been as colorful as his boastful opponent's.

It was Smith, however, whose pen shaped the only reality available to us of the confrontation of two cultures, and he often saw what he wanted to see. He wrote as much to defend himself from critics conscious of his lack of social status and excessive ego as to tell the truth. Also he hoped to promote the colony in England, to convince others that this wilderness was well worth the conquering. At least he did write, and there are few other accounts of his encounters with Opechancanough.

Smith quickly forgot his meeting with Opechancanough and grew anxious to explore the rivers of the Chesapeake Bay. As the colonists became desperate for food in the fall, he was appointed supply officer, giving him the chance to look for Indian villages that would trade corn for "trifles." Soon he decided to explore the shallow, torturous Chickahominy River which empties into the James a few miles above Jamestown. His first journey was surprisingly successful, for he encountered two hundred Indians carrying more corn than he could carry on his barge. A second trip reaped an equally abundant harvest of corn.

But in November 1607, the colonists wanted still more corn, and Smith offered to go, anxious to finish his "discovery" of the river. Taking the pinnace, then transferring to a barge and finally, as the river narrowed, to a canoe rowed by two Indians, Smith made his way up the Chickahominy with two white men. Taking one Indian with him, he ventured into the swampy woods and stumbled right into an ambush. Finding himself surrounded by two hundred men with bows and arrows, he tried to escape, using the Indian as a shield, but the river would not let him. As he wrote, "minding them more than my steps, I stept fast into the quagmire." Thus he was captured and taken to Opechancanough.

Smith decided to try exploiting Opechancanough's ignorance to save himself, especially since he was told that the men left at the canoe had been murdered. He presented the chief an ivory compass and proceeded with a "discourse of the roundness of the earth, the course of the sunne, moone, starres and planets." This may well have been the ideal subject for regaling a man with some kind of Aztec background. Certainly Opechancanough seems to have been charmed, feeding his well-guarded prisoner liberally and pumping him for information about ships and sailing. He too offered tales of the course of the river, how "within 4 or 5 daies of the falles, was a great turning of salt water." Meanwhile, Smith grew very friendly with his guards, acquiring a knowledge of Indian ways that would later foster the colony's survival.

That winter was exceptionally cold, but the weather did not deter Opechancanough from touring with his talkative prisoner among the villages on the many rivers north of the James. Eventually he led Smith to Werowocomoco, residence of Powhatan. As an unarmed, defeated prisoner, Smith was the first Englishman to meet the chief werowance.

Smith's facile imagination proved equal to the encounter, however. To account for the English presence on the river, he spun an elaborate story. The English ships had been defeated by the Spanish in battle and thus forced to retreat into the Chesapeake Bay. There they met friendly Indians who advised them to go up river for the fresh water they needed. Unfortunately, a boat began to leak and so they had to anchor at Jamestown and wait for Smith's father, Captain Newport, to come help repair the ships. (Smith felt certain that such a connection with Newport would help his cause.)

Powhatan nodded, but he was not buying it yet, for he wanted to know why the English traveled to the Fall Line. Smith then said that their motive was revenge, that Newport had had a child slain by the Monacans. Clearly Smith had learned much about why and with whom Powhatan battled.

After Powhatan assured Smith that he would be glad to avenge the child's death, they began swapping stories. Powhatan wove a few about a salt sea upstream where cannibal tribes lived, and beyond them, men in short coats with houses of brass. In return, Smith told about Europe and its glorious battles, many won by Newport, the "King of all the waters" with his bravery verified by the loss of an arm in combat. Perhaps John Smith should be celebrated as the first creator of American fiction!

After considering these stories, Powhatan had Smith dragged out onto the ritual ground and prepared for execution. But little Pocahontas, then maybe eleven, claimed the prisoner as her own, and he was saved at the last moment. What exactly happened and why has never been clear, but Smith was soon "adopted" by Powhatan and freed. Now he too was a werowance, and in a sense, brother to Opechancanough. In return he promised Powhatan a grindstone and two "great guns."

Smith was in even greater peril when he returned to Jamestown. Blaming him for the deaths of the two men on the Chickahominy, President Ratcliffe promptly sentenced him to die the next morning, and then declared that the colony would be abandoned. But that evening Captain Newport sailed in and stayed the execution. Possibly Powhatan had delayed Smith until the ship was sighted coming up the river. If so, he saved Smith's life and helped hasten the end of his own people.

In the spring and summer of 1608, Smith finally was able to explore the rivers of the Bay. His status at Jamestown had risen as others died or left, and he was next in line as president. In the meantime, he could get in no trouble "discovering" the rivers. Although he met many Indians and captured all kinds of food and goods, Smith did not encounter Opechancanough on this voyage.

Probably Smith was relieved to confront the open hostility and childlike cunning of the Indians instead of the masked and convoluted machinations of class-conscious English snobs. His bravery must be acknowledged, however, for few others would dare voyage up unknown rivers in the wilderness. He coolly appraised the rivers' fitness for navigation and easy food of fish or fowl, calculated the number of fighting men along the banks, and accurately mapped his route. There were no raptures about riverine beauty or promise of gold for this pragmatic adventurer, though he did continue to question Indians about a sea beyond the mountains. Likewise, he set out to know the Indians even better, so that he might beat them at their own power ploys. It did not hurt that his luck held or that Opechancanough kept his distance.

Smith had good reason to question the superiority of English civilization, especially when he saw men dying because they were unable or unwilling to cope with the facts of the wilderness. He had carefully noted Indian customs that ensured their survival but his advice was rejected by the colonists when he returned. Suspecting that the river water at Jamestown was unhealthy, he urged the summer dispersal to higher ground, but that was interpreted as weakening political cohesion. The English also would rather go hungry than adopt the alien diet and fishing techniques of the Indians.

Eventually, though, Smith brought the colonists to understand that nature would not yield her bounty without much effort on their part. As president of the colony, elected in September 1608, he was finally able to force them to make some concessions to nature and Indian ways so that they might live, but it was not easy: "had they not been forced nolens volens perforce to gather and prepare their victuall, they would all have starved and have eaten one another." He refused to solicit more corn from Powhatan's sparse reserves, for this dependence had spoiled the English. Instead, he demanded that they work before they could eat, reminding them that "this Salvage trash you so scornfully repine at, being put in your mouthes, your stomacks can digest it." Any person who failed to gather as much food as Smith did would be "set beyond the river, and for ever bee banished from the fort: and live there or starve." Since Indian knowledge of nature was to be used, men were "billetted among the Salvages, whereby we knewe all their passages, fieldes and habitations; how to gather and use their fruits as well as themselves." For a brief time, then, both groups shared the river. Some adoption of Indian ways, even if under duress, did pay off with a lower death rate. But resentment against Smith's highhanded ways lingered.

Smith had not forgotten the abundant harvests of the Chickahominy and Pamunkey River Indians, and his men were still hungry. To get through the hard winter of 1608 when the rivers were frozen, Smith took fifteen men to trade with Opechancanough. Again they found themselves surrounded by warriors with bows and arrows, not corn. This time, though, Smith was a legitimate leader, so he took the offensive, scolding Opechancanough for not sharing his plenty:

Opechancanough, the great love you process with your tongue, seemes meere deceit by your actions. Last yeare, you kindly fraughted our ships; but now you have invited me to starve with hunger. You know my want; and I, your plenty: of which, by some meanes, I must have part. Remember it is fit for kings to keepe their promise.

Opechancanough seemed to agree with this reasoned eloquence, but he insisted that the men wait overnight while more supplies could be brought. But the next morning what appeared were several hundred well-armed Indians.

Smith was undaunted. As one of his men later reported, he firmly issued a challenge to Opechancanough to join in naked, single-handed combat, to be appropriately staged on an island in the river. The winner would take all. The ploy had worked with the Turks; perhaps it could with these aliens.

Opechancanough stalled, perhaps either astonished at Smith's reckless bravado or unable to take the challenge seriously. This was definitely not his style of military strategy. An impatient Smith grabbed at the Indian's warlock, holding the hair as he pointed his loaded pistol. This scene has been memorialized by an artist in an edition of Smith's *General Historie* with a caption reading, "C. Smith taketh the King of Pamaunkee prisoner." Somehow, though, the tall, stalwart Indian looks relatively undismayed, backed up by his warriors. However, Smith reports that Opechancanough was intimidated, and he and his men submitted to this display of nerve and firepower. Whatever happened, the corn was forthcoming. Smith makes little of an Indian attempt on his life as he rested a few hours later or of later attempts, reportedly planned by Opechancanough, to poison him. Somehow Smith had prevailed.

Ironically, it was the river he had first explored that played a role in Smith's downfall. On a summer 1609 expedition to the Falls, Smith realized that after a flood had forced the soldiers to higher ground, Captain West had restored his fort to the river floodplain. By this time Smith understood well why the Indians set up their camps as high above the river as possible. He then purchased the Indian village on the nearby hill and named it Nonesuch for its "pleasant and delightful view." When he told the soldiers to move, they objected rather physically, forcing Smith to return to his boat. Smith was barely gone, and in fact, his boat had grounded a short ways downstream, when the Indians successfully attacked the riverside fort. Hearing the noise, Smith returned and forced the recalcitrant soldiers back to the hill location.

At that point, Captain West returned and belligerently moved his soldiers back to the river. Exhausted by the proceedings, Smith returned to his boat and fell asleep as they sailed, holding his powder bag on his lap. Somehow a spark fell and the bag burst into flame, tearing his flesh "in a most pittifull manner." Smith jumped into the river and almost drowned in his pain (possibly neither he nor the other colonists knew how to swim). The burn was so severe that the sailors did not expect him to survive the trip to Jamestown for medical aid. He did, but bedridden by his wound, he returned at the end of his presidential term in September 1609 to England, never realizing that he would not see Virginia again. His pen would have to serve the cause of the new world instead.

Smith's departure proved a significant loss to the struggling colony. That winter, sickness, starvation, and Indian attacks claimed the lives of many colonists. The recuperating Smith was denied the pleasure of seeing his strategies for coping with the wilderness vindicated. But he had set the mold for the native heroes who were to come out of the American wilderness, as John Seelye points out, men who would share "his courage, his cunning, his ingenuity, his faith in the future, his utilitarianism, and his generous way with the truth." They would also share his obsession with rivers, "a mixture of quixotic idealism and expedient means, greed licensed by a sense of destiny." His map, far more a river than a land map, would guide many more up the rivers he had begun to wrest from the Indians. He left an indelible mark on the future of the river he had known such a short time.

BATTLING FOR POSSESSION

THE LORDLY Opechancanough did not abandon his fight for the river lands when his worthiest opponent retired from the scene of battle. For several years, he led the English to believe he was friendly, and even on the verge of conversion to Christianity. It was he who witnessed the wedding of Pocahontas to John Rolfe, a gesture of conciliation. If he ever regretted the Indian maiden's early attachment to Smith and then Rolfe, he never showed it to the English. But he had not retreated. The last insult evidently came when his friend Nemattanow was killed by the colonists, who had laughingly dubbed him Jack-of-the-Feather. By then Powhatan had died and Opechancanough had "grasp'd all the Empire to himself," as Beverley put it, skillfully manipulating the strings he held.

Just before noon on Good Friday, March 22, 1622, a carefully laid plan began on signal. All along the river at each of the new settlements, the Indians, visiting casually, suddenly massacred almost 350 English colonists with their own weapons. Jamestown itself had been warned, however, because an Indian boy revealed the plan to a white man who had "used him as his son," as Smith reports, and he quietly rowed across the river in the darkness to alert the Jamestown people.

Now that the Indians had disclosed their devilish and ferocious nature, the colonists had no hesitations about open warfare, especially since they no longer needed Indian corn. What followed, as they killed almost twice as many Indians in the next few weeks, were called battles, not massacres.

The biggest Indian killer of all would prove to be the white man's diseases, especially smallpox. Still, the next twenty-five years on the river were ones of blood and fire. The pattern was fairly consistent. English soldiers would burn out Indian villages, forcing the people back from the river. In turn, a group of warriors would attack the more isolated settlements; then the soldiers would burn more villages. It was not exactly a war, but a series of guerrilla skirmishes and ambushes.

By 1644, Opechancanough was ancient, at least a century old, confined to a stretcher and unable to open his eyelids. But he was not defeated yet, and he planned and brought off yet another massacre. This time at least five hundred colonists were killed, but there were enough settlers in Virginia by then so that the impact was small. Finally, he was captured by the English in 1646 and brought to Jamestown where he was put on display. Proud to the end, he informed the governor that had he been the captor, he would not have humiliated him so. Soon afterward, the old man was shot in the back, joining in death his old enemy, John Smith, who had died in his bed in 1631 at the age of 51.

The river would twice more be seen as a battleground in the years to come, but never again would the question of ownership be at stake. The Indians, now considered subjects of the English king, were limited to clearly defined "reservations" (the English word for "waste ground") far from the James. The new tenants, no longer captive to the dream of a golden river, did not write letters home praising the river for its fluid beauty and the varied life it sustained, only

The Indian massacre of 1622, from T. de Bry's *Voyages*
(1624 edition). — *Virginia State Library*

for how it could further their dreams of wealth. This shift in perspective can best be measured by looking at another outsized knight, the Atlantic sturgeon who ruled the shadowy depths of the tidewater river for almost three centuries after John Smith left for England.

The sturgeon came from an ancient line, from a species dating at least 120 million years. If the Indians had any notion of a river god, it must have been centered on this magnificent and ugly, bony-headed and armored beast. For three or four thousand years, multitudes of mature sturgeon had left the salt water of the Atlantic Ocean to find fresh shallow water where they could spawn, and they often tracked into the James, possibly going far beyond the Falls. Though their upstream run began in the spring, it could last throughout the summer. Yet there were springs when for some reason relatively few sturgeon traveled up the James.

The Falls must have glinted silver in the sunlight when these fish crowded in, for they were giants that could reach twelve feet and six hundred pounds, though more commonly they were less than half that. Those colonists who later claimed that a man could cross the river on their backs at the Falls were perhaps not exaggerating, for these rather lazy bottom-feeders were known to pause for naps at midday. But they were not as vulnerable as it might appear; fish hooks and nets of the time were generally useless against their armored strength.

Historian Robert Beverley in 1705 described how the Indians traditionally captured this prize of the river. One way, probably favored by the young warriors, was literally man-to-fish combat. When a fish swam into a narrow portion of the river, up streams or between rocks, to forage for food by burying its pointed snout in the mud, it would be welcomed by an Indian with a strong noose woven out of reeds which he used to lasso the fish's tail. The fish, naturally, would struggle vigorously, and the Indian would have to hold tight, catching hold of the gills if he could; "that man was counted a cockarouse, or brave fellow, that would not let go till with swimming, wading and diving, he had tired the sturgeon and brought it ashore." A less energetic Indian might take his dugout canoe into the river, hoping that a sturgeon would leap in, as they often did, and that the boat would not sink before he towed it to shore.

The sturgeon could also be speared, but it had to be relatively quiet first. A favorite ploy was to make a hearth in the middle of a dugout canoe with a fire which would "dazzle the eyes of the fish" as well as illuminate the bottom of the river more clearly than daylight would allow. At each end of the boat would be an Indian with a spear, gently poling along to surprise any fish attracted by the flames and then darting them. Beverley does not say how the prize was hauled in.

There are reports from a later date of Indians clubbing to death the fish between the rocks of the Falls, for by then they had learned the wasteful ways of the white man. Previously, Indians had taken only what they needed or could preserve, using some ingenious ways of preserving the fish—ways now lost to us, such as turning it into a flour suitable for bread.

The colonists were astounded by the sturgeon when they arrived in May during the spawning run. But, typically, their primary interest was in how these great fish could be turned to profit, not used for food. Their first report asserted that "our fishing for Sturgeon cannot be lesse than 1000 pound sterling a yeare." Visions of easy wealth from caviar and isinglass danced through their heads. They sent for fishermen from England, and lamented their lack of salt for preserving the roe better.

The sturgeon run turned out to be a feast or famine situation, and the English did not understand how to take advantage of either. Repeatedly they did have "great store" of sturgeon, but Smith reported that "our men would so greedily surfeit, as it cost many their lives." More likely it was the river water that was costing lives, for the sturgeon were most easily caught when the river was lowest in the summer, and thus most apt to be contaminated at Jamestown. The "sweet flesh" of the sturgeon did sustain the earliest colonists through some hard times, as Smith proudly recorded that only seven men died in June and July of 1608 because they lived upon dried sturgeon; they had caught "more sturgeon than could be devoured by dog or man," according to other reports. Under Smith's direction (using Indian fishing techniques), the colonists took all the sturgeon they could get that summer, at one time pulling in 52, at another 68.

Caviar began to look like the most promising source of wealth, for even then Londoners paid high prices for the Muscovy product. Captain Samuel Argall was dispatched to the colony to harvest sturgeon in 1609. There was a catch, though: no salt, no refrigeration, and no facilities to convert the roe into caviar. The warm climate of Virginia meant that preservation was a problem, one not encountered by the Muscovites. Evidently, at least three returning ships did carry loads of sturgeon roe which deteriorated en route to England even though they were boiled and pickled. Tobacco, on the other hand, needed no preservation and so would ship much better. Thus Virginia lost its opportunity to have an economy based on caviar.

Another factor in the abandoning of sturgeon as a source of profit was the unpredictability of the runs. If the sturgeon came in the spring of 1610, the colonists were unable to catch them. William Strachey wrote that, "The river which was wont before this time of the year to be plentiful of sturgeon has not now a fish to be seen in it, and albeit we laboured and hauled our net twenty times a day and night, yet we took not so much as would content half the fishermen." He put the blame squarely on the ineffective fishing practices, though, and not on the fish: "let the blame of this lie where it is, both upon our nets and the unskilfulness of our men to lay them." The Indians could have told the English that nets were not the best way to catch sturgeon, but then the Indians were content to make do with fewer fish.

Once the sturgeon could no longer be considered as a commercial crop, the colonists literally ignored them. They were unwilling to struggle with these unpredictable beasts for food they did not know how to preserve. The Indians were gradually forced away from the rivers, so they too encountered the sturgeon no more. For two centuries it looked as if the fish had won by default and essentially had the river all to themselves most springs.

But the time was to come—after dams were erected in the Falls that blocked the now invisible sturgeon from part of its freshwater spawning grounds—when the white men began to see that the market for caviar was still strong, and shipping the roe was no longer a problem. So began years of slaughter, when the roe were stripped from the great bodies and sent to New York to be made into caviar. In one year, 1880, over 100,000 pounds of sturgeon were "harvested." A brochure written in the 1890s called the sturgeon a "lumbering, stupid" fish "who really doesn't care enough for the vanities of life to fight his way out of the nets." The king had lost his dignity and prestige and taken on a new name; he had become "James river bacon."

The tidewater sturgeon fishery did not die out until the 1930s, since isinglass from the air bladder and oil from the head proved almost as valuable as the roe for a long time. Today the sturgeon rarely bother to venture upstream. Deterred by pollution and dams, they still lurk in the ocean and the Bay, waiting to return. A few small ones occasionally brave the changed river, but they are often dead when they are discovered.

Ironically, had the colonists' attempt to harvest the sturgeon roe been successful, the story of the river might have been different. No one would have dared block the progress of the fish, and the river's health might have been guarded more zealously if profit had been involved. Yet perhaps not.

Each spring I hang over the 14th Street Bridge railing, hoping that maybe this year I will spy the silver of one of these giant fish, finally returning to its old spawning ground, perhaps even its birthplace. I grieve for the disappearance of "royal fish" from the river in my time. In dreams I picture myself crossing the river, not on a bridge but by lightly stepping on the broad backs of the sturgeon, warning the ancient kings of the river about the nets and lines they must avoid and break.

THE RIVER AS SHAPER

THE STRUGGLES between Indians and white men, or between men and fish, are actually only a small, though dramatic, part of the story of Americans and their rivers. Yet these scenes, permeated by language of warfare and profit, of antagonists intent on conquering, defending, and defeating to gain wealth and glory, are the ones which are replayed in most historical records. The ideal they proclaim of men in battle with nature, trying to assert their power over its more unruly and unpredictable aspects, has become part of our American heritage.

It is difficult, therefore, to see that beneath the frantic action called history lies another, less visible drama of people gradually responding and adapting their lives to the shapes and rhythms of their environment, especially to the moving waters they chose as their highways. And beyond that, in the background, is the slow-motion saga, most visible to geologists, hydrologists, and geographers, of how the rivers have kept on creating the landscape that people claim as their own.

For eons the river has been a shaper, continuously molding the landscape as its waters transport soil and carve stone.

Though to the short-lived creatures on its banks its works seem to be indelibly etched, the river erases as much as it creates, never ceasing the deliberate process of sculpting along its sinuous length. Like Proteus, the water god of myth, the river is both shapeshifter and transformer, art and unconscious artist.

Seen from above, it seems frozen eternally in relief sculpture, a bright ribbon edged in green which weaves its way between hills and through the floodplain of contrasting squared-off fields. But the essence of the river's art is motion, not the illusion of permanence. It is the crafting process lying behind the artifacts of stone, wood, and curve which man sees that gives them a live beauty, transmuting them—for some of those people on its banks—into the poetry that sings of birth, the grace of aging, and death.

There is nothing haphazard about the shaping of any river, although accidents of nature and constructions by man play their roles. The course of every drop of water is governed by natural laws whose logic can be expressed by the classic symmetry of mathematical equations. Americans who have abandoned the seventeenth-century belief in divine providences recognize no artistic, metaphor-making consciousness who is deliberately carving with flowing water intricate moral lessons in stone and soil. However, there is undeniably complex but consistent designing to be found in the river's art.

The processes that shape the James shape all rivers and their landscapes. They begin with raindrops falling on the hills. Some soak into the ground, sinking into the aquifer and perhaps later erupting into springs that feed the rivers, and others simply run off the land, carrying loosened topsoil and weathered rocks into gullies and streams. Drawn by the relentless pull of gravity, the raindrops move downhill, heading toward their mother ocean, forming the brooks, rills, and creeks which soon join to make the river. Each stream labors to contour the land, whether into the V-shaped valleys that divide mountains or the rounded slopes that roll over the piedmont, as it rushes to sea level.

The watery fingers of the James have smoothed down one towering mountain range and are now caressing the slopes of another. They have chiseled caves and the famed Natural Bridge out of limestone and coral laid down by ancient seas. They have given two cities, Lynchburg and Richmond, their "Roman" seven hills to boast about. Above the Falls, wherever there is shape and leveling of the uplifting earth, the sculptor responsible has been the James and its tributaries.

Even though rivers are tugged by gravity and the sea, they rarely follow a direct path to their destination, for that is not the way of least resistance. Water, like most people, would rather ease around an obstacle than bore through it. From this simple preference can come elaborate, regular meanders, snaking over the floodplain like sine curves, a process best seen from high above rivers like the Mississippi.

On the more resisting bank, called a point bar, the river deposits some of its load of silt and rock as it flows by, while its currents sweep under to scoop out the opposite bank. When the neighboring land is relatively level and soft, the resulting bend can keep extending toward its eroding elbow until it hits the resistance of harder rock or hill; then it reverses its pattern to begin swinging back to the other side of the valley. Sometimes the river silts up the ends of a former bend to form an ox-bow lake or a gut. After years of twisting in its bed, the river flows through a wide, rich plain of leveled soil which is subject to drowning by ocean and flood. Bordering the plain may be terraces, remnants of more ancient floodplains, which are often faced with cliffs or worn into hills.

Judging from the wide floodplain stretching along the river above the Falls, the James was slithering restlessly, weakly imitating the Mississippi's patterning, for centuries before the most recent uplift of the earth. But now it has been "rejuvenated" again, as geologists used to say, corralled by the rising land so that it runs down a straighter course to the Falls, making islands out of the most stubborn obstacles. There are few scars or ox-bow lakes remaining from this river's earlier braided and meander pattern in its plowed and forested plains.

Downstream, however, only the water level has risen recently, not the land. So the James retains and keeps pushing at a few great meander loops, now punctuated with guts and swamps, remnants of past river paths, and manmade gravel pits. The processes of deposition and erosion continue, though on a smaller scale, below Jamestown where the tidal currents assert their full power and the river widens. Meanwhile the former peninsula of Jamestown has become an island, losing many feet of river bank that the colonists farmed along the deep harbor where their ships anchored, and houses dot the growing sandy beaches across the river on the inside of its bend. But it is on this diminishing island and the broad tidewater curves where the story begins of how the river helped determine the course of a new nation.

Even before the colonists left England, it appeared that the rivers, especially the James, would be the center of their new world. For generations the maps drawn of Virginia were dominated by the exaggerated shapes of rivers, creeks, and bay. Gradually the waterways assumed more realistic proportions, but known details of the river's contours remained pronounced. As late as 1755 a French map of Virginia and Maryland painstakingly displayed virtually every size of stream, although the western portions were somewhat speculative. The settlements spread along the banks seem to be lost in this extensive network of watery highways.

To see the river as the first Virginians did, for as long as two centuries, I have to readjust my vision, put it into re-

63

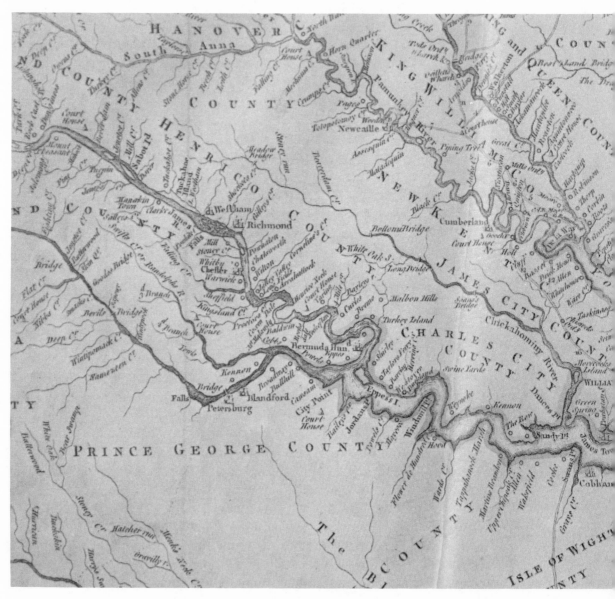

Section from the Fry and Jefferson map (1775) showing the bends and curls of the James.

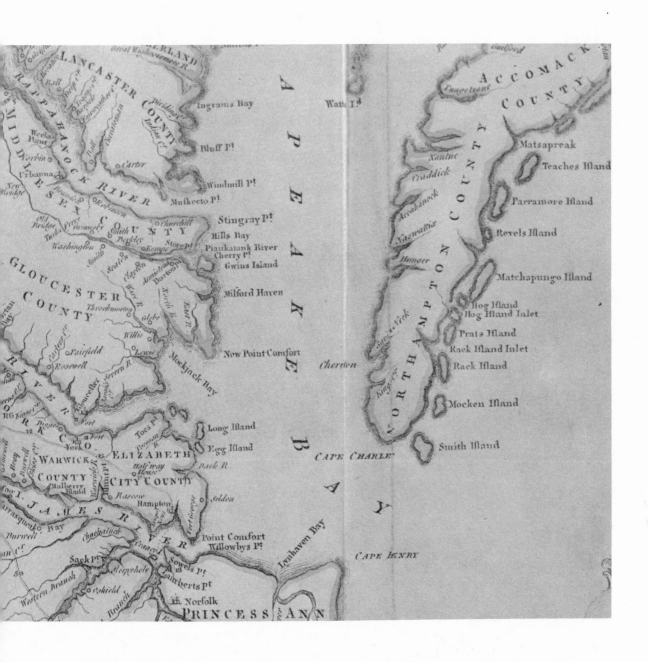

verse. Then I can see a world balanced on the fulcrum of running water, ordered by land broken by occasional clearings between the tall green shadows of forests. My focus must be on the surface, as was theirs, barely noticing the current which persistently swings around growing land points and under eroding banks. Aside from oysters easily reached or masses of spawning shad, I must forget about the life teeming below that surface. I am now looking at an indispensable highway, one which both divided and connected, partially molding a people's culture as it had the earth on which they lived.

Moving out from Jamestown proved no easy venture for the English, more because of the Indians who had to be displaced than the currents or the bends. Yet almost from the beginning, they kept leaving the relative safety of the Jamestown fort, where bickering and sickness often prevailed, for the calmer spaces stretching along the cleaner water upstream. They preferred the fields already cleared by the Indians, either buying them with beads or copper, or burning out less reasonable groups. The big river bends, or what they called curls, above the junction with the Appomattox were particularly appealing, even though sailing ships had trouble maneuvering the twisting river with its shifting winds and channel. But here, on land repeatedly enriched by floods, the English felt particularly safe, protected by the river on most sides and a barricade at the neck of land. They must not have noticed how easily the Indians moved over the water in their primitive but effective dugout canoes.

Such a place, on Farrar's Island at Dutch Gap, was in 1611 the site of a new town. Here the dictatorial Sir Thomas Dale set up the town of Henrico (also called Henricus and Henricopolis), naming it after another English king. Within four months, powered by enforced threats of torturous death, the men had erected two or three streets of "well framed houses," including five houses on the riverfront reserved for "the honester sort of people" who would "keepe continuall centinell for the townes securitie," according to Beverley. A church, a hospital, and a college for converted Indians were also built or planned. Further up the river, above the curls and below the Falls, an iron furnace was built on Falling Creek with the aid of cooperative Indians hoping for protection from the presumably ferocious Monacans upstream. Nearby were several farms, including Varina where John Rolfe developed the golden weed with tobacco seed from the West Indies and later brought his Indian bride, Pocahontas.

At least twice the river colonizers had to retreat to Jamestown, leaving their lands to later and luckier settlers. Settlements all along the river, including Henrico and the Falling Creek mines, were abandoned by the few survivors of the 1622 Indian massacre. The next Indian attack in 1644, aimed mostly at farms south of the river, left other prime land cleared for a while. But the repeated contraction to Jamestown seemed only to release greater energy for new settlement, clearing the way for newcomers to the colony. They included some Cavaliers fleeing the uncongenial politics of Puritan England who acquired large grants for tobacco plantations. After the 1646 treaty, the Indians had to give up all their claims to the river below the Fall Line. The Powhatan tribes were forced to settle beyond the York River on the north and behind a line equally distant from the river on the south side.

However, the upriver Indians were getting restless, especially since they were being pressed by belligerent raiding parties of Iroquois and Susquehannocks. The English, keeping to the terms of their treaty, joined forces with the Powhatans against their old enemy when the Monacans came down the river seeking refuge from the raiders and alliance. They found war instead. A creek just below the Falls may have been the only winner of the battle that followed in 1656—it gained the appropriate name of Bloody Run. The Powhatan chief Tottopotomoy and a hundred of his warriors died, as did many British soldiers, and Colonel Edward Hill returned to Shirley Plantation in disgrace. Although the Monacans were theoretically the victors, they soon disappeared up the river and lost their place in history as a tribe. And the white men became even more determined to rid their land of the Indian menace, now embodied by raiders from "foreign" tribes who kept attacking the more isolated settlements up the river.

Twenty years later, the war against the Indians served as the basis for the first revolt against British rule, but again the river had the last word. In 1676, the hot-headed young Nathaniel Bacon, owner of Curles Neck and a Falls plantation, recruited colonists to go up and down the river seeking pockets of Indian resistence. However, he was far more interested in toppling the British governor, William Berkeley. Berkeley could not deny his own policy of Indian conquest, but he tried in many ways to strip Bacon of the militia power he had acquired. The confrontation came at Jamestown, where Bacon barricaded the sandy beach that connected the peninsula to the mainland. Forced to drink the brackish well water of Jamestown, the English soldiers capitulated, forcing Berkeley and a few loyal gentlemen to flee in ships downriver. Jamestown was burned, but it had not claimed its last victim—Bacon soon died in Gloucester County, apparently from what was still called the "Jamestown fever."

Later a Virginia historian, Charles Campbell, would argue that the fate of the Indians was sad but justified, since "perpetual possession of this country by the aborigines would have been incompatible with the designs of Providence in promoting the welfare of mankind." Nature's treasures of fertile soil, minerals, and metals would have been "forever entombed" without the energy and implements of the white man. Navigable rivers, "the natural channels of commerce," would have "failed in their purpose had they borne no freight but that of the rude canoe." Yet by depending heavily on the river simply as a highway and ignoring the Indians' reverent and detailed knowledge of the river's ways, the white men gave up a certain degree of control. The tidewater river would shape their developing society just as surely as it had shaped the land.

HIGHWAY AND BARRIER

BY THE middle of the seventeenth century, the colonists could turn from the struggle to survive to the serious business of establishing their own social and economic system along the navigable river, now freed from the Indian threat. For a time they accepted the natural upper boundary of rocks at the Fall Line, and built their houses, first of wood and then of brick, along the curves of the lower James. What resulted was a linear structuring of class and wealth strung along the region they called the Tidewater, a name signifying the centrality of the river in their lives.

The most enterprising newcomers gradually secured large grants stretched along the more fertile soil close to the river, often by using the land rights, called headrights, of the poorer emigrants and indentured servants they had transported. There they established plantations, and as servants completed their indentures, the planters turned increasingly to slaves for the cheap labor needed to grow as much tobacco as possible and quickly, since this crop exhausted the soil in a fairly short time. Soon the river had taken on its nickname, the "old muddy Jeems," as the red dirt increasingly eroded. But they did more than break up the soil.

Since the major highway was the sometimes unpredictable river, planters soon found it useful to have virtually every kind of craftsman available on their land. Each large plantation, then, became a fairly self-sufficient settlement under one management, linked by its boats and wharves with other similar plantations, and particularly with England.

Back from the river far beyond the choicer soils were white people who had more trouble eking out an independent living, the yeoman farmers, many of whom were once indentured servants. By the eighteenth century, access to the river was generally denied to them, so they also had little access to the wealth being shipped on the water. Crops for the profitable export trade usually had to be sold through the nearest plantation owner with a wharf. Many of the more enterprising farmers, especially south of the river, eventually gave up and went to North Carolina to be free of the power of the river barons.

People with the privilege of living on the river had a decided advantage, in spite of the occasional danger of floods. On the river banks were to be found the cooling summer breezes, the easy fishing, and more fertile acreage, but particularly a front row seat on the colony and the world. The river was swarming with boats and ships of all descriptions by the eighteenth century, many built right on the plantations from their own forests. Indeed, some of the earliest plantation owners had first been shipwrights and sailors and were still unwilling to venture far from the water which had given them a good livelihood. They benefitted from the many ways England encouraged shipbuilding (in response to her own lack of timber), exempting Virginia-made ships from duties and pushing the emigration of shipbuilders. By the time the British shipbuilding industry began demanding protective legislation, first passed in 1680, it was too late. The colonists kept on building, now devoting more of the ships to internal use, plying the James, the Bay, and the West Indies.

Shirley Plantation, as seen from the river.—*John Theilgard*

For a long time, the native boats on the James were either versions of the serviceable Indian canoe or shallops, shorter and with masts, both of which could navigate the creeks and shallow river stretches with ease. Every owner of riverside land had at least one, to fish and go oystering, transport tobacco out to larger ships moored in the channel and bring the goods back, even to attend the parish church in many cases. By 1648, hundreds of boats were reported tied up on the James, and many had been built on the river.

By the eighteenth century, much of the shipbuilding had shifted to public shipyards in seaport towns, especially Norfolk, but boats, particularly those suited to the river's variable depths, were still being built on plantations such as Flowerdieu, Westover, and Berkeley. The variety of these crafts shows how river-dwellers adapted to the shapes of their rivers and creeks: there were canoes, bateaux, barges, punts, piraguas, flats, pinnaces, shallops, and sloops. Sloops were particularly popular, even after England restricted Virginian shipbuilding; they were built in the colony, filled with tobacco, and sold off—complete with cargo—in the West Indies. Since they had to dodge pirates in the Bay and the Caribbean, they were developed for speed and maneuverability.

The people with access to boats also had access to what money could be brought in by the tobacco trade. They could best afford the treasures of Europe and the Orient brought by European ships to grace their new mansions. They also supported the New England ships that carried loads of slaves to work the tobacco fields and cargoes of rum from the West Indies. Those who lived away from the river highway had no such opportunities. Ironically, then, the ability of riparian owners to communicate by boat with each other and the rest of the world eventually erected considerable barriers of class and wealth between them and their neighbors.

Yet even with their boats, the widely separated plantations were probably less connected with each other than
each was with England. The river, with its tides, strong
currents, and unreliable winds, could be a rough highway,
especially for smaller boats. Whenever there was visiting
between plantations, people planned to stay for a while;
thus, the famed hospitality was also a necessity. But even
the river-dwelling planters were slow to evolve into a com-
munity, especially as compared with their New England
counterparts.

The river made and shaped the fortunes of many gentlemen in the eighteenth century, but few were as colorful and
articulate as William Byrd II, builder of the manorial Westover. Like most of the wealthy planters, he inherited much
of his land, more than 25,000 acres including the key river
lands above Jamestown and along the Fall Line, from an in-
dustrious father and grandfather who used politics and indentures freely to acquire property. But he developed his
extravagant tastes, as well as a gentleman's education, in
England where he spent most of his first thirty years as a
gallant bachelor. For a while, the James meant little more to
him than a highway link to England, the center of civilized
life. But he came to relish the role of riparian lord, enter-
taining lavishly and at length whenever he was not crossing
and exploring up the river, seeking new land grants and resources to develop, especially metals.

Much of our knowledge of the social structure of the
time as well as of natural history comes from Byrd, especially his *Natural History of Virginia*. Herein are many hints
about the key role of the rivers in shaping the society developing along them. As he declares, "no land on the whole
surface of the earth is as well situated as this one is, because
it is completely irrigated with numberless beautiful large
rivers abounding in ships. . . ." The rivers provide abundant fish and easy commerce "right in front of the houses of
the merchants and planters," thus saving "much trouble and

expense." In the same paragraph where he praises the waters as "extremely pleasing and sweet," he notes that such "easy and convenient" navigation means that hundreds of English ships come, selling Negro slaves and buying tobacco. In fact, the tobacco would be virtually worthless without the possibility of world trade. He clearly understood the economic value of the river.

Not the least of the river's gifts which Byrd praises is its fish life. Byrd lists species at length, spotlighting the ones which taste best. Sturgeon, he claims, tastes "like the best veal"; he particularly lauds the abundance of spawning fish, especially herring, for "it is unbelievable, indeed, indescribable, as also incomprehensible, what quantity is found there." He seldom found himself at such a loss for words, but it is, finally, our loss, for it is impossible for us to visualize today what he saw.

The little book gives testimony that the river was thoroughly a part, even a center, of the life beside it, contributing to the wealth of those with access. One wonders about those who could not benefit from this resource, but that is a world which Byrd knew little about. Whenever he did encounter people without a river, as in eastern North Carolina (a place he facetiously named Eden), he is scornful, finding them lazy and provincial.

But the days of the wealthy planters were numbered, largely because their sons and grandsons lost interest in farming the money crop of tobacco at about the same time that the land's riverborne fertility became exhausted. Byrd himself died in debt, but it was his son who actually lost much of the river land. An era of concentrated river wealth soon passed, but not without leaving its divisive mark.

There were other kinds of division enforced by the river. A look at a map shows that rivers have always been natural boundaries, dividing nations, states, parishes, and neighbors of all sorts, human and animal. No number of bridges, for example, will change the fact that the Mississippi divides the whole country, not just physically. What were once rather formidable physical barriers, even though penetrated by ferries and bridges, often linger to mark cultural and psychological boundaries today.

The James very nearly splits the state of Virginia in half, zigzagging from its headwater springs northwest in the mountains near what is now West Virginia to the southeast corner of the Chesapeake Bay. As long as the river was used as a highway in the thick wilderness, however, people stayed close beside it and north was rarely divided from south. The Indian confederacies above and below the Fall Line paid little mind to the river as a boundary. Tribes like the Weyanoke and the Monacans established villages on both sides. The Fall Line rapids and the mountains did raise serious barriers, but not the river itself. Perhaps it was so much at the center of the Indians' lives, especially during the fish runs, that it could not be easily perceived as dividing.

That unity was threatened when Jamestown—and eventually the entire north side of the river—was chosen to be the hub of the new colony. Even after most settlers, including governors, chose not to brave the legendary Jamestown sicknesses, its place of preeminence in the colony was assured by its busy wharf, first on the Back River and then, when that filled up, on the deep water of the river curve where ships could be moored to the trees. For many years, every European ship coming up the rivers of Virginia to trade had to stop first to register at Jamestown. Naturally, many simply chose to load and unload their goods there, thus making Jamestown an economic center. For easier access, by road if necessary, both to the assembly and the trade, official institutions such as courthouses and churches of the counties and parishes that stretched across the river and even the College of William and Mary were set on the north side. When Jamestown was finally abandoned at the end of the seventeenth century, the capital moved only a few miles north to Williamsburg. No one evidently even considered a south side location. This division proved to be irreversible.

It took little time for the southsiders to begin developing a different sort of culture, one centered more on farming and raising hogs than on politics. Their major early contribution was the use of marl as fertilizer, and not the production of political pamphlets, even during the Revolution. Wealth and power were increasingly concentrated on the north side, especially after roads were cut to connect plantations on the many navigable rivers above the James.

There are different ways to measure this growing domination of the north side of the tidewater James, but my yardstick is a family one. In 1608 Captain John Woodlief came to Jamestown, learned how to survive, and returned to England to gather his family and indentured servants. Selected to be governor of a settlement above Jamestown on an 8,000-acre site named the Berkeley Hundred, he brought a shipload of new colonists late in 1619. Upon arrival, he conducted what Virginians now proudly cite as the first Thanksgiving service. As often happened in the colonies, Woodlief's ability to produce profits for his financial backers came in question and he was fired, so he moved south to land along Bailey's Creek and the river near present-day Hopewell.

Meanwhile, Benjamin Harrison settled in Surry County, right across the river from Jamestown. He prospered as a tobacco planter, leaving wealth that enabled his grandson to purchase the Berkeley Hundred, thereby moving into the circles of colonial power on the north bank. His son, Benjamin Harrison IV, married the daughter of wealthy planter King Carter and built the manorial house next door to William Byrd's Westover, beginning his dynasty there. Struck down by lightning, he left Berkeley and its wealth to his son Benjamin, freeing him to become a prominent colonial statesman, first as a burgess and eventually as a member of the Continental Congress and signer of the Declaration of

Independence. In turn, the "signer's" youngest son William Henry and great grandson Benjamin were both to become Presidents of the United States after they had left Virginia for the more promising West. The house still stands as a symbol of a Virginia plantation dynasty, with its vanishing claims to aristocracy.

Captain Woodlief's descendents across the river, by contrast, are almost erased from history, having continuously but obscurely farmed their river land until it was lost in the Civil War. Younger sons migrated not to the centers of power at Jamestown, Williamsburg, or even Richmond, but primarily to southeastern North Carolina, looking for more fertile soil. They were never baronial planters or political leaders, but many were reasonably successful farmers, respected and influential in their rural communities south of the James.

The growing division in interests and prestige between the two banks of the river grew, especially as connecting roads were cut on each side. The developing split can be mapped in Charles City County, just above Jamestown, which originally stretched south of the river from the North Carolina line to the Appalachians and north to the York River. By 1655, Francis Lutz writes, "inhabitants of the sprawling territory south of the great natural barrier saw no reason why they should be compelled to travel a long distance, including the crossing of a turbulent stream, to attend church and county court sessions." They resented the periodic militia musters on the north side, but not as much as did north side residents who feared they might be called on to "protect the distant frontiers."

People did not accept the river as a political barrier without a struggle, however. The General Assembly regularly mandated public toll ferries, to be regulated by the counties, to promote unity within the colony. Convenience was another reason for ferries, but trade itself was little affected, being more oriented to the big ships in the river channel which served boats from both sides. In 1705 there were twenty public ferries operating on the tidewater James and its main branches; by 1748 there were thirteen more.

In spite of the ferries, the river remained a formidable physical boundary. Most ferries could not operate with any regularity, especially without motors, on a river with strong tides and currents. Also, ferry owners were entitled to build ordinaries, or taverns, to put up "travelers, who, on many occasions were unable to cross the stream for days because of storm and high waters." Since the ferry owner could make far more money at his tavern than with the low tolls, he had little incentive to keep his boat moving on schedule. Charles City County, like the other counties spanning the river, first divided the parish, since church attendance was considered crucial, and in 1703 completed total political division, splitting off Prince George County to the south.

This division of tidewater society became more pronounced in the nineteenth century, especially after the Confederacy died. As Parke Rouse puts it, "Below the James lies Dixie." Southside Virginia has remained relatively poor and uninfluential; the growing of peanuts, pine, tobacco, and hams has brought little profit and less power. The area has a high percentage of Afro-Americans, yet it is also a stronghold of white Anglo-Saxon Protestant laborers and of fervent conservatism. "Southside" has retained a character which some denigrate as "redneck fundamentalism" and Rouse calls "stubborn, old-fashioned, slow-paced, insular, ready to fight at the drop of a hat." All seem to agree that in many respects it is far more like the deep South than the north side is. The division of Virginians initiated by the river still lingers, though it is slowly yielding to bridges and the wealth promised by new industry.

Maps can show how the river has physically woven its pattern through the landscape, both uniting and dividing its

banks. But the social patterns the river has inadvertently encouraged and shaped from the beginning are more subtle,
though almost as persistent. The reality of the river plantations and their stratified society has turned into a myth,
cherished by tourists nostalgic for what seems to be a more
ordered life. As they look out over the green lawns on the
north bank, they see only the placid surface of the broad,
muddy water. Since they look from land and not the river,
they miss seeing how this powerful and sometimes disor-
derly river helped shape that order as it did the land. The
early struggle to adapt a society to the river is as hidden as
the currents and tides which push against upstream travel
and slowly shift soil from one bank to the other.

IN RIVER TIME

A PHOTOGRAPHIC INTERPRETATION
BY JOHN THEILGARD

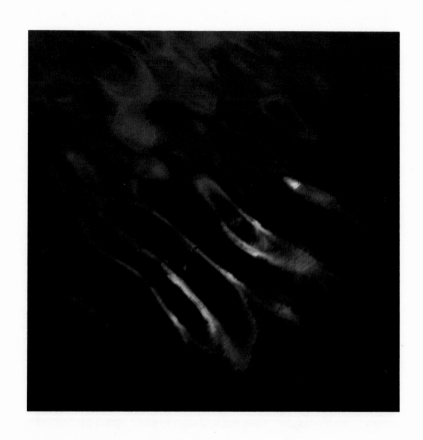

13

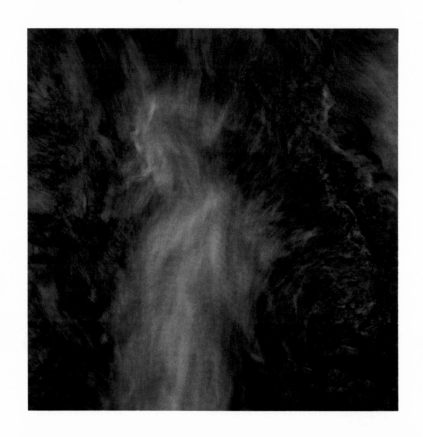

MOVING UPSTREAM

IN SOME ways, the river of the wilderness has never been domesticated, even today, in spite of the idyllic picture painted in tourist brochures. Replace boat engines with muscle power against erratic winds and currents, especially if the boat is pointed upstream, and it becomes clear who is still master. But the myth is seductive, enough so that my daughter and I decided that our first canoe trip on the James should be on the river curls below the Fall Line. We naively anticipated an afternoon of easy paddling and a picnic near the early site of Henricopolis.

The only wilderness we saw as we put into the waters warmed by a coal-fired power plant at the gap were the thickly wooded, isolated banks and a few waterfowl who rose at our approach. Nature seemed friendlier than the motor boats and barges which left wakes that threatened to tip our canoe. The curious stares of the boaters made us feel like intruders in their rightful territory. With some relief, we beached on the shallow side of a bend.

The upstream return was another story entirely; the wind had come up and both tide and current were against us. As we launched toward the channel, a sharp wind caught us and we found ourselves struggling for footing in two feet of soft eroded mud. Chilled, muddy, and grateful for shallow water, we climbed back into the canoe to fight our way upstream. It was not easy, for we advanced only a few inches with every hard paddle stroke, and the wind kept pushing us backwards and sideways. The wood debris piled on shore was now threatening, for it left no alternative but to keep paddling.

We were justifiably frightened and frustrated as we inched near the boat ramp, but we also found ourselves unaccountably exhilarated. Though I do not plan to repeat that particular drama, the image of our battle with the current often flits across my memory, and it is not unpleasant. Now I understand why those new settlers would keep pushing up the river, even while longing to go with the downstream flow back home.

By 1700 the frontier was still just upstream a ways, in the more hostile world of granite, islands, and rapids above the tidewater. In July a ship sailed into Hampton filled with 207 Huguenots, exiled for years from their cozy, prosperous villages in France, who hoped to build a French Protestant town in the Norfolk area. They were welcomed by Governor Nicholson with disturbing news; their destination had been changed and they were to go up the James. William Byrd I, inheritor of land in the Falls area and influential in the colony, had had the last word on their fate. They were to settle in the wilderness above the Fall Line, securing that land for the white man.

The omens were all foreboding at Jamestown where the prospective settlers had to transfer to smaller boats that could negotiate the curls. The town had recently burned for the third time and so had been abandoned as a capital. Sickness was still prevalent, and many of the French proved as vulnerable as the earlier settlers. As they learned more details about the requirements of survival on the frontier, especially without a navigable waterway, they became even more apprehensive, for their skills were those of business, not farming. Not surprisingly, many chose to desert here. Only 120 trusted themselves to the small boats and the currents of the James. Almost immediately a boat that was filled with goods sank, claimed by the rough waters.

This last leg of the voyage, overcast by dread and illness, must have been the worst. They passed the site of an earlier settlement called World's End, made the left turn into the Fall zone, and landed at the tiny trading outpost of rude houses around Shockoe Creek. Loading what was left of their supplies onto borrowed wagons, they trudged through the thick forests, following a faint path more than twenty miles into land long ago cleared by the Monacan Indians on the south bank of the river. Their ears still rang with the rushing of water over granite that would block their boats from the outside world of commerce. But the key to their survival lay in the unusually fertile floodplain of that same river.

It was a desperate fall and winter as the ill-prepared settlers used up their meager supplies, especially when another group of more than a hundred Huguenots arrived in October expecting to find a thriving town. Friction developed between the leaders, meaning that the new group had to hack out a settlement several miles downstream. Soon, though, Byrd and Governor Nicholson proved their support by soliciting charitable donations throughout the colony. The ensuing generosity proved justified, for within a year the French had learned to be adept farmers, growing fruit and fat cattle on their bottom land, and establishing trade, not warfare, with neighboring Indians.

Although plans had been drawn for a French-style village around a central square, with outlying farmland along the river, these never proved practical. The fertility of the piedmont floodplain encouraged the Huguenots, like the Monacans before them, to live more separately than they had intended, becoming a segmented agrarian society which stretched back from five miles of river bank. In time, they too lost their cohesive identity by intermarrying and moving to other rivers. They opened the way for settlement of the piedmont, but today there is as little trace of their half century of settlement as there is of the Monacans' longer tenure.

The man who had directed the Huguenots to the James River frontier, William Byrd I, had done much to establish the character of the Fall Line region. He was what we would today call a "wheeler-dealer," a man who thrived on trade and not the more placid agricultural rhythms. His inherited location at the head of navigation and beside the river's rapids was an appropriate focus for his energy. He began at age eighteen, with 1,800 acres south of the Falls, and his uncle's stone house. To that he added thousands of acres, largely by using headrights of indentured servants. He built the only flour mills for miles and large warehouses. To fill the latter, he sent out trading caravans to bargain with the Indians through the Carolinas, then shipped tobacco, furs, and Indian corn to England. He not only shipped back English goods and servants, but Negro slaves, rum, and molasses.

His son, the master of Westover, had grown up far from the rough-and-tumble world of the Falls, and he had other plans for the vast acreage around the Falls he had inherited in 1705. Being an absentee owner of farms and coal mines suited his temperament much better than trading. But the pattern was already set. It took him more than twenty-five years, but he finally recognized that the area was "naturally intended for Marts, where the Traffick of the Outer Inhabitants must Center." After Major Mayo laid out the street plan in 1737, Byrd nostalgically named the new town Richmond, for somehow he was reminded of Richmond on the Thames. Perhaps Byrd was a "reluctant father" of the city, as Virginius Dabney says, but the nature of the river had again had the upper hand and shaped history.

William Byrd II was not particularly impressed by the wild beauty of the Falls area, according to his journal. He wittily characterized the roar of the water over the granite as a "Murmur loud enough to drown the Notes of a Scolding Wife." His interest in this part of the river was solely practical, not aesthetic, as he figured out how to build canals to his mills and to mine iron ore from the large river island then called Broad Rock. For him the sculptured rock of the James was no more than a nuisance for shipping or a convenience for powering mills. He would offer no rapturous descriptions of its massive beauty.

Upstream settlement and trading grew quickly, as restless newcomers, inspired by the Huguenots' success, lay claim to the more than a hundred miles of piedmont floodplain above the Fall Line. Although there were those who managed to patent large grants of land along the river, including some who, like Thomas Jefferson's father, had dreams of establishing tidewater-style plantations, the settlement pattern was again dictated by the river. The floodplain may have been wide and fertile, but the shallow and rocky river prevented the large scale navigation which had ensured the wealth of the tobacco barons. Frequent floods were a deterrent to growing crops, as was the fact that the region was not threaded with navigable creeks and small rivers. In short, it was a different sort of river requiring different styles of adaptation by the white men, just as it had from the Monacans. The energetic freshwater stream with varying levels, supporting much less fish life except in the spring runs, ruled decisively against a repetition of the tidewater design.

The river did direct the path of settlement, but the pattern that emerged above the Fall Line was neither linear nor layered, as it had been for the Monacans and tidewater Virginians. It was more a series of relatively disconnected intersections along the river, radiating generally north-south from the river's overall east-west direction. The centers were located at the junctions of major Indian trails, used not so much by Monacans as by the more restless hunting tribes, which in turn had followed in the tracks of wild animals, especially buffalo. The river at these points was often fordable, which meant that ferries were also feasible.

By the time the white men began moving up the river in any numbers, the Indian threat had diminished. Most of the Monacans had moved away from the contested river lands of their fathers after the Indian military campaigns of the seventeenth century, for they were farmers, not warriors. But one part of the Indian heritage proved invaluable for people coming to this part of the river: the dugout canoe. A platform made of boards lashed against two giant canoes could be a barge that could be poled almost all the way to the trading center developing at the Falls. Similar unwieldy boats could also serve as ferries to connect the great trails, even at high water. So by 1748, there were as many as nineteen ferries licensed to operate above the Fall Line, and an equal number of settlements on the verge of being declared towns.

The two busiest trading centers developed at the two points where the river took sharp turns. Scott's Landing, later to be Scottsville, was situated at the northernmost point of the river on a great horseshoe bend, more than fifty miles above Richmond. Soon Lynchburg was incorporated near John Lynch's ferry at the next bend of the river, another fifty miles upstream. Both towns became launching points for the intrepid folks seeking to penetrate the mountains through nearby gaps. The river might not have been very navigable at that time, but its direction was the one land-hungry people pursued as they pushed back the frontier.

Inevitably Virginians became increasingly frustrated with the rocky barrier in their river highway, especially those who lived upstream. One who pushed for clearing the route was the Reverend Robert Rose of Scott's Landing, dabbler in law and medicine, owner of vast acreage on two upper tributaries, the Piney and the Tye rivers, and inventor of a bateau for transporting tobacco downstream. The General Assembly accommodated him by passing a law that provided for "more effectual clearing of the James" in 1745, although nothing would be done for twenty years. The shallow channel below the Falls, where upstream silt collected, forced larger ships to unload at Warwick, just above Falling Creek but six miles from the Falls, so it was not just rocks that blocked the way. But there was still hope that the river highway might soon be cleared. In 1768, when the indebted William Byrd III sold the rest of the Falls land (30,000 acres) in a lottery, he promised that "obstructions through the falls and other parts of the river will shortly be removed. . . . Thus, communications will be open to the western frontier of the middle colonies and to the Ohio." He did not mention just how this feat was to be accomplished.

Rather soon it became clear that the river would not be easily tamed, not even by the canals that the General Assembly kept mandating. In May 1771, torrential rains poured down on the Blue Ridge portion of the river basin, though downstream residents were enjoying a sunny spring. The river began rising, up to sixteen inches an hour for sixty hours. The result was a wall of water, as much as 40 feet high, sweeping across the Fall Line. Behind it, engulfed in the raging waters, were houses, cattle, and trees, soon joined by warehouses, hogsheads of tobacco, and even ships loosed from their moorings. According to one anonymous reporter, it was as if "Old Nick had bored a Hole through the Mountains, and let in the South Sea upon them."

At least 150 persons died in what may have been the highest flood ever on this river. Those who survived found themselves in a changed landscape: the floodplain of Richmond was swept clean, islands had become sandbars, and

The horseshoe bend of the James at Scottsville. — *Scottsville Museum*

the tidewater curls were rearranged, acquiring up to 12 feet
of sand topped with flattened rocks. In 1772, an obelisk was
erected on Turkey Island below Richmond, standing 45 feet
above the river's normal level where the flood peaked, which
still declares:

> The Foundations
> of this PILLAR was laid
> in the calamitous year
> 1771
> When all the great Rivers
> of this Country
> were swept by Inundations
> Never before experienced
> Which changed the face of Nature
> And left traces of their Violence
> that will remain
> for Ages

It would not be the last catastrophic flood on the James,
though it may be the highest recorded, especially for the entire river, and the most sudden. Some property losses were
reimbursed by a sympathetic Assembly. The river itself
quickly adapted to its new shape, and after the maps were
drawn again, most people forgot what the old shape looked
like. But those who had experienced the fury of the flood
were skeptical that their temperamental river could be tamed
in any way, even with canals. Still, memories of the flood—
if not the monument—were erased almost as quickly as the
wounds of the land healed.

Any notion of battling the river was soon eclipsed, for
another sort of war was sweeping across the ocean and upstream to Richmond, now the capital of Virginia. The river
would give shape and scene to the crucial last act of the
Revolutionary War; the struggle to control the land would
again center on the river.

The British did not try to venture up the river until the
turn of 1781, when they aimed for the soft underbelly of
their colonial empire so they could finish off the length-

ening rebellion. They knew well that up the river lived Thomas Jefferson, architect of the Declaration of Independence and present governor, and possibly many Tory sympathizers who prided themselves on their Cavalier heritage. They also hoped to destroy the stored tobacco and munitions in Richmond which were supporting the drawn-out war.

Earlier, the British felt they had adequately blocked the James without having to travel up it. Norfolk had been captured and burned on January 1, 1776, and the Hampton Roads area was further secured in May 1779, when a squadron of 1,800 men on 22 transports arrived. Over a hundred vessels, the remnant of the Virginia navy, were captured or destroyed and all the towns were taken and plundered; the fleet withdrew without losing a single British soldier. But the war went on.

For the river, this begins as a story of fire and ice but little death. At Suffolk, the Nansemond River which empties into the base of the James was literally set afire in 1779. On the wharves were hundreds of barrels of tar, pitch, turpentine, and rum which "descended to the river in torrents of liquid flame," according to historian Charles Campbell. Strong winds fanned and floated the "splendid mass" across the river "in a conflagration that rose and fell with the waves" and burned acres of marshlands. It was not to be the last fire seen on these waters.

The following winter the James and much of the Bay were effectively blockaded, not by a colonial navy but by ice. Ever since the first days of settlements, Virginians had known some unaccountably severe winters when their navigable waters were frozen solid. So it was in 1779, when even the Bay at Hampton Roads turned into thick ice from shore to shore. The river would offer no other barriers to the invading British, however.

The traitor Benedict Arnold met little resistance from the river or colonial militia when he sailed up the James with his British troops at the turn of 1781. He moved quickly, before Jefferson could prepare any opposition. Landing at the Westover wharf, he took his men by land to Richmond. Major Simcoe took a force to Westham to destroy the foundary and ammunition and, incidentally, throw five tons of gunpowder into the river (most of which would be later recovered by the hard-pressed Americans). Jefferson had meanwhile crossed the river to refuge in Manchester. Arnold sent him a letter proposing a deal: leave the river free for British vessels to come and take tobacco from the warehouses, and Richmond would be spared. Jefferson refused, though there was no way his militia could effectively blockade the river, so Richmond was burned. Again no blood was shed.

Returning to his flotilla at Westover, Arnold proceeded to sail back to Portsmouth. The outnumbered American troops followed along the river's banks, paralleling the British force, but they were effectively barred by lack of ships or bridges.

Having determined that the James made much of eastern Virginia vulnerable, the British prepared a campaign for the spring that would exploit their naval advantage. A small group of American boats collected in March at Turkey Island, but morale dropped and many men deserted; there was no pay, not even in grog. In April Generals Phillips and Arnold again set off up the river. Arnold surprised the new naval force which was waiting at Osborne's at Dutch Gap for French reinforcements. Again he offered a deal if the Americans would give up their ships, but was refused. Seeing their doom, the colonials scuttled or burned most of their ships and swam to safety across the river, retreating by water. The British proceeded to the Falls, but they hesitated to cross the river there, even though they had a bigger and better force, for now they were confronted by fire from Lafayette's troops. Instead, they looted Manchester, then destroyed the village of Warwick a few miles downstream. As they moved, American troops followed on the north side, too weak to attack but strong enough to enforce the river barrier.

Since the Virginians had been totally unable to protect themselves from British assaults coming from the river, they decided in June 1781 to move their military stores upstream to Point of Forks, where the James (then called the Fluvanna to that point) intersected with the Rivanna. Baron von Steuben had several hundred recruits guarding the depot on the south side of the James. The British Major Simcoe, coming up on the north side, was blocked without enough boats to cross the river. So he resorted to a ruse: his men stretched out along the banks and built many campfires. Steuben, convinced that he was faced by the entire British army, retreated south, and Simcoe sent men over in canoes to destroy the abandoned stores.

The British did have ships in the lower James in July 1781, so when General Cornwallis received orders from General Clinton to send his troops from Williamsburg to Portsmouth and on to New York by water, there seemed to be little problem. But when Lafayette saw the preparations, he decided to attack the British rear guard at Green Spring, downstream from Jamestown, after most of the troops had crossed the river. Cornwallis anticipated the maneuver and held back the bulk of his army. This time, without the river as buffer, there were heavy casualties on the American side. Rather than pressing his advantage, Cornwallis chose to move his men quickly over the river at Jamestown, so they could report to New York as ordered.

In September the French fleet arrived to support the Americans, bringing some most welcome rum. Almost every small boat, barge, and even canoes left near the James gathered at Burwell's Ferry near Newport News to form the "Mosquito Fleet." Two boats which had been sunk for concealment from the British were raised and restored. Meanwhile, Washington and the French army had cornered the British troops under Lord Cornwallis in Yorktown and forced the surrender which effectively ended the war. Though various skirmishes between ships would take place in the next eighteen months, especially with pirates and freebooters still roving the Bay, the James and its new country were safe from invasion for a while. The Virginians took note of their river vulnerability, learning that whoever controlled navigation could control the land. They were determined to be prepared in the future.

THE CANAL TO
THE WEST

FOR MONTHS in 1983, the water gates were clamped shut, holding back the river to expose several miles of an earthen ditch, remnant of a dream called the James River and Kanawha Canal. I picked my way among the half-buried sewer pipes and earthmoving machines, following in the digger's path, to look for discarded treasures—once junk—of more than a century ago. It was a quiet Sunday, with city sounds muted by cliffs on one side and marshy river bank on the other. With some imagination, I heard instead the creaking of iron hinges on the locks, cries inciting mules on the towpath, and the laughing echoes of excursioners floating up to Lynchburg. My concentration was interrupted by the imperious blast of a train whistle. I backed into a quarried niche in the cliff, perhaps carved out long ago by a rented slave, to retreat from the cloud of dust flying off an interminable train carrying coal from the mountains to the sea. Now the gates are opened and the detoured flood rushes through again, going nowhere except back to the river, a truncated reminder of the American hope of conquering a frontier wilderness by taming its rivers.

Even before the American Revolution, George Washington started preaching the advantages of building canals to lead the young country westward. In theory, it seemed a simple enough matter to bypass the river where it raised navigational barriers, to borrow its water but not its swift currents to flow through a deep ditch with locks where mules could provide the power. Then the river's water would provide a proper highway, not so subject to the moods of weather. The same arguments were soon to be heard all over the country, and they were to be bolstered by the easy construction and quick profits of the Erie Canal.

However, when Washington took his proposal for two canals crossing the Fall Line, one on the Potomac and one on the James, to the House of Burgesses in 1774, it was rejected—it would cost too much money and it did not appear practical enough. Besides, it seemed to be a matter for private investors, especially since the state was not inclined to negotiate the resulting political squabble between northern and central Virginia canal advocates. But once independence was achieved, the idea of "river improvements" became more alluring and the canal fever spread. Americans were ready to turn their backs on England and move westward; a people who had challenged one world power and succeeded were not to be intimidated by the obstacles of a mere river.

The projected canal appealed to the westering vision by offering stronger political and economic union with the west and a foothold on possibilities for America to fulfill its "manifest destiny" of stretching to the Pacific. But Virginians were more impressed by the opportunities the canal would open for making money at home, thus keeping restless workers from ranging to the richer lands of the west. James Madison, writing to Thomas Jefferson about Washington's "patronage of works for the extensive and lasting

improvement of natural advantage," listed the possible benefits for Virginia. Such works "will double the value of half
the lands within the commonwealth, will extend its commerce, link with its interests those of the western states, and
lessen the emigration of its citizens by enhancing the profit-
ableness of situation which they now desert in search of
better."

What started out to be a fairly modest plan to circumvent
the Falls soon became part of Washington's dream of "The
Great Central American Water Line." With canals and highways, where necessary, to connect the James to the Green-
brier, the New, and the Great Kanawha rivers, linkage could
then be made all the way to the Rocky Mountains, following the Ohio, Mississippi, and the Kansas rivers. Though
the full project never materialized, it does show the kind of
grandiose schemes Americans were inspired by their rivers
to concoct. Again the myth of the river obscured the reality,
for no one dreamed of the cost and difficulties that were to
arise in the next fifty years.

The James River Company was incorporated in 1785 and
within a decade two canals had been built around sections of
the Falls. Although they did not yet connect with the tidewater river, they showed significant profits after full tolls
were put on in 1806. Many of the rocks were cleared from
the river above Richmond and wing dams were constructed
which would channel the current in shallow stretches. This
allowed the passage from Lynchburg to Richmond of bateaux, each powered by an expert steersman to shoot the
rapids and two strong polemen to defy the current; by 1816
some could even make it through the treacherous Balcony
Falls from Buchanan by shooting rapids and dodging rocks.
The trip was quite risky at both high and low waters, and
the James is often one or the other, but the profits to be
made from selling tobacco, iron ore, and furs in Richmond
were convincing.

For a while only freight could make the journey between

Lynchburg and Richmond—seven days down and ten days back. To pole these unwieldy craft was a choice occupation for Negro slaves, in spite of the physical rigors. It was hard not to feel free on the river, away from an overseer, pitting brain and muscle against an indifferent adversary, the changing and rocky river. The bateaux traveled in groups of three; two were usually sold to the lumber-hungry Richmonders, then the polesmen spelled each other back up the river in the remaining craft. At one time, five hundred bateaux were challenging the river with their profitable loads.

A bateau ride was no trip for passengers, however, and there were many on the lower James who wished to visit friends and family who had moved west. The consensus was that only a full canal could provide a dependable, calm waterway. But the longstanding rivalry emerged over which bank should have the canal. Southside residents justly feared that profits would remain only along canal borders. But no less a speaker than Patrick Henry (ironically, hired by a Manchester merchant who feared competition) opposed them in the General Assembly. For years they petitioned for the "healthy competition" of a Manchester canal extension, but they could never buck the power of the north, and so had to be content with their short canal at the base of the Falls.

After many lawsuits were filed claiming that the James River Company, then the biggest business corporation in Virginia, cared only for its dividends and so neglected necessary repairs and improvements, in 1820 the state purchased the company's charter. Unwilling to antagonize the powerful stockholders in the corporation, the state promised to pay a 12% dividend rate each year until 1832, and 15% "forever afterwards." (Washington and Lee University long received $3,000 a year from the state for the hundred shares of stock willed it by George Washington, even after the canal was defunct.)

Taxpayers were no happier with results of the state's supervision either, once they saw how much money was required to build and improve the half-finished canal. Now that it had become a political matter, sections of the state which did not benefit opposed the canal loudly. The divided legislature eventually refused funds, so in 1835 it was time for the canal to go back to private ownership. Americans have rarely been satisfied with their business arrangements: under private ownership, the canal made too much profit, but state ownership meant that too many tax dollars had to be spent.

After three years of raising funds, the James River and Kanawha Company was in business. By 1840, the canal, at a safe remove from most of the river and now accommodating the mule-pulled packet boats, had been completed to Lynchburg, and in 1851 all 197 miles of canal (with 37 miles of slackwater river) were completed to Buchanan. The canal, forty to fifty feet wide and five feet deep, had proved to be a massive venture, requiring 90 locks lifting 728 feet, 23 feeder dams, 12 aqueducts, 198 culverts, and 135 bridges. Next on the list was a 1,900-foot tunnel which would bore through the mountains west of Buchanan, but that was abandoned after 1.5 million dollars were spent.

There were also unexpected physical problems with the James River Canal. Design and management of the construction were haphazard and amateur, as verified by engineer-architect Benjamin Latrobe, who observed in 1796 that the canal "is neither judiciously, nor ornamentally managed, and there are several most gross blunders in its execution." Construction proved quite hazardous, with only black powder and hand labor to clear the way. The toll in human life was high, but the numbers are not recorded, for they were the uncounted lives of rented slaves and later, Irish immigrants. Eventually at least 11 million dollars were spent just on construction of the canal from Richmond to Bu-

The James River Canal, near the mouth of the North River. Watercolor
by Edward Beyer (1858). — *Virginia State Library*

chanan, fifty miles beyond Lynchburg and the Blue Ridge. The price for improving the river with a canal had proved far greater than anyone had imagined.

Taxpayers were also surprised to discover that the temperamental river made maintenance an ongoing and expensive process. The clay lining the canal often leaked and eroded the bank facing the river, called the berm. Floods washed out banks, locks, and towpath, and the usual summer droughts literally grounded the boats, necessitating the building of dams to channel more water into the canal. And so the fish met even more barriers. Each disaster fueled the "progressive" argument for replacing the canal with the railroad.

While the country bickered over its division into North and South in the 1850s, many people delighted in cruising the canal from east to west in packet boats seventy to eighty feet long and eleven feet wide. For a little over five dollars they could make the 33-hour journey from Richmond to Lynchburg, stealing through forests and farmland. Quarters were close, especially at night, but as George W. Bagby recalled, daytime lounging on the deck, "where there was a great deal of interest, and naught to mar the happiness," was particularly enhanced for gentlemen by the freedom to "spit plumb into the water" at will, reinforced by juleps from the "vigorous and healthy" bar below. Ladies also enjoyed strolling on the towpath between locks as a welcomed antidote for cramped "limbs."

However, even at the height of activity, there were only six passenger packet boats operating. The profit lay in transporting goods, not tourists. Over 200 freight barges were in constant use, carrying lumber and agricultural products east, including plenty of corn whiskey from the mountains, and ferrying general goods and staples west. Barge crews would even tie up to help a farmer finish his harvesting so they could fill up with wheat for mills at the Falls. In 1860, the peak year, almost a quarter of a million tons of goods were barged east and west.

Even racial differences counted for little when the common enemy was the fury of the river. The ancient rock bounding the river where it passed through the Blue Ridge Mountains at Balcony Falls had proved impenetrable, so canal boats had to pass through so-called slack water. In 1854, a boat with fifty people aboard was inching up the towline in flooding waters when the line broke and the boat was hurled over a dam and into the rapids, where it hung tentatively on a rock. Three slaves and two white men came to the rescue, fighting the rapids to tow the passengers ashore, but Frank Padgett, the slave who led the successful rescue, and another slave were drowned. The boat's captain later erected a granite memorial to Padgett's bravery, which still stands.

Any kind of union promoted by the canal could not compete with the increasing disunion of the nation. The Civil War began the canal's doom, for all work and improvements stopped abruptly. In 1865, General Sheridan and his troops wrecked the waterway locks and banks for ninety miles above the Falls, and the great Richmond fire burned the central offices. After the war, federal funds for canal repair were not available for the defeated state, in spite of enthusiasm for rebuilding from the midwest as well as a French company which owned land in western Virginia. A flood in 1877 finished off the half-repaired canal for good. Few complained when the railroad purchased the canal to use its towpath for the railroad bed. No one cared about navigating up the river any more, for the romance of the railroad was now ascendant.

In the summer of 1983, however, it was a railroad conglomerate, including the railroad still running on the towpath, which was responsible for literally unearthing memories of the days of the canal's prosperity. In the heart of Richmond at the foot of Capitol Hill, the CSX Corporation began digging for the foundation of a skyscraper to overlook the James, right on the former site of the great canal turning basin. Here was once the heart of the canal system, where barges exchanged goods with ocean-going ships, but it was filled long ago to become valuable downtown property. CSX, realistically motivated more by public relations strategy than by guilt over the railroad's role in the canal's demise, halted construction when bulldozers began uncovering mud-preserved canal boats.

Time and money were short, but scores of people descended on the site with buckets and shovels when the state archaeologist called for help through the media. Soon they found over thirty boats, including three in good enough condition to attempt salvaging. They also found piles of 1850-vintage junk—shoes, lamps, tools, garbage—whatever was either thrown out or had been sunk in the basin. In a few weeks, the bulldozers had to start up, leaving more treasures in the mud, but for a while the city shared a trip into the past. The boats, including the oldest canal boat ever recovered, lie in a restored segment of the canal awaiting funds for preservation and exhibition. For historically minded Virginians—and they are legion—the canal is still not entirely dead.

It lives in a more tangible but less obvious fashion in the pattern of settlement existing above the Fall Line. The canal itself is virtually invisible, little more than a shallow ditch, long claimed by silt and weeds. But its effects linger. Its path is marked by the towns on the north side, some with fine houses and marketplaces still standing, which now struggle to survive, too far from the interstate highways. The south bank of the river is largely inaccessible, for its rolling hills covered by farmland and forests lack even a road to parallel the curving river. Thus the canal reinforced the sort of cultural division begun by the tidewater river.

The upper James, though, shows few marks of its busy past today. Since development became centered north of the canal, generally on hills safely above most flood levels and not on the river itself, its banks and floodplain are relatively free of the kind of land improvements of business and industry common on most rivers. Even houses are rarely visible from the river between Lynchburg and the Fall Line, and upstream between Buchanan and Balcony Falls. A few vestiges of the earliest river improvements, such as wing dams and ditches that fed the canal, remain, but one must look sharply to see them. Thanks to its canal heritage, the river runs freely and rather clearly in these stretches, no more a highway but a one-way trail reserved for canoeists seeking an easy float through a predominantly natural riverscape.

FLOATING THE
UPPER RIVER

THE IDEAL way to float the upper James, according to my "river rat" friends, is in a tractor-tire innertube, either alone and soundlessly or with a group of boisterous friends, pulling extra tubes with coolers tied inside. That is, it is ideal for those who do not object to their skin being broiled on one side and shriveled and bruised on the other. Evidently there are many who are willing to trade their comfort for the privilege of knowing the river so intimately. On almost any summer day when the water is low and clear, the young at heart can be found bobbing through sections of riffles between Buchanan and the Fall Line. In the rapids that foot each of the favored stretches are their more daring compatriots, testing themselves in whitewater canoes and kayaks against the river's more challenging obstacles at Balcony Falls and in the heart of Richmond.

However, I prefer the meditative company of the lazy canoe floaters, paddling to break the monotony of flat water or to dodge rocks and islands, but most of the time simply dragging an oar as a rudder and letting the river current have its way. I also feel akin to the fishing floaters I pass who are absorbed in casting for the wary smallmouth bass. For contemplative canoeists like us, floating means there is no where to go, and no when either, for the space of a day or a weekend.

Admittedly, floating is not as effortless as it sounds. Cars and canoes must be shuttled over back roads. Parking at isolated landings may be hazardous; one Saturday night the battery disappeared from my car. Also, the resolve to float and not to paddle often fades in response to the thrill of negotiating the next set of noisy riffles downstream. Sore muscles and aching joints seem inevitable for all except the athletic or the incurably meditative. No matter, a float now and then is worth any trouble.

Many find that the upper reaches of the James, where the shallower water courses over the limestone laid by prehistoric seas in the shadow of the Blue Ridge Mountains, offer the best canoeing or tubing, especially in the brilliantly tinged autumn. Much of the charm is that so few people trek over winding mountain roads to this relatively secluded valley far from the highways. Even fishermen prefer to go for the trout in upstream tributaries or for the smallmouth bass downstream, leaving the river free for the select folks who simply enjoy it.

The more than fifty miles of piedmont river between Scottsville and Richmond include the stretches that keep drawing me, however. Here are gentle curves, multicolored rocks sometimes rising above the water, and islands of all descriptions. This is a world in motion, never the same. Its constant variations in water level and clarity combine endlessly with the changing reflections of light, wind, rain, and season. Even the islands keep adjusting in shape from year to year, expanding on one end as the other yields to the currents, and some dividing or disappearing after high water times. This shifting land will not be owned, regardless of deeds lying in county courthouses, except temporarily by campers with boats or deer giving birth in the spring, and the ever-present kingfisher who so raucously claims his territory.

My favorite camping spot is a sandy sculpture garden south of the Hardware River junction, which can be reached now only by canoe. Here, in eons past, mineral-enriched rock of varying hardness was melted and literally poured through the granite. Then the water began persistently carving out all the weaker points. The result is art, unique sculpture of many shapes and textures streaked in red, yellow, and blue, which is visible when the water drops its veil. Thoreau's words come to my mind, for it is "as if, by force of example and sympathy after so many lessons, the rocks, the hardest material, had been endeavoring to whirl or flow into the forms of the most fluid." Each stone seems almost as liquid as the river which has shaped it, like flux caught in a moment of solidity.

I do not linger long here, for it is the river which takes shape over hidden rocks that keeps luring me downstream. The fluid patterning and sounds of the water's surface make complex music. The underlying rhythms are smooth and swift, with harmonic changes rung by fluctuating water levels. The melody comes from below, where the uneven contours of the river bed make the whirls, eddies, waves, holes, and smooth or rippled textures. Counterpoint is rung on the surface with the instruments of wind, rain, and the dipping and skating insects, punctuated by the percussive leaps of the frogs and the fish. Once, as I paddled in a rainstorm, jumping with each distant thunder clap, I heard under the pounding raindrops a low steady hum which penetrated and calmed my shivering body. I can still hear this hum of the river's "valv'd voice" in my dreams, and I wonder if it might be the same soul that Walt Whitman invited into his body in "Song of Myself." Perhaps, for me, it is.

With practice, I have learned to read the river, to imagine with some accuracy what lies beneath the designs spreading over its surface. This is a skill necessary for running white-water rapids or finding the fish hovering in the rocks' eddies, but I use it more to anticipate the next musical phrase of the river. There are also times when I have learned to suppress this knowledge, to give in for a while to the hypnotic spell of the watery world, my soul detaching from time and responsibilities. It is then that I understand myself what Thoreau meant about drifting: "I almost cease to live and begin to be. A boatman stretched on the deck of his craft and dallying with the noon would be as apt an emblem of eternity for me as the serpent with his tail in his mouth. I am never so prone to lose my identity. I am dissolved in the haze." During these timeless moments I succumb to the spell of entropy, caught in the fluid time which melts trees and rocks. But I must not forget that the music of rocks and currents is the same siren song which lured mariners to their doom.

Actually I am not in much danger, for I am never alone in my canoe. My favorite partner, my daughter, is a silent paddler who lets me roam mentally but keeps me pointed safely. Few sounds of the twentieth century distract us, only the faint drone of a plane, a tractor, or a train, all easily drowned by riffle splashes. The trees lining the river block any view of house or barn above the floodplain, and the cows browsing beneath are not intrusive. So I let myself free to float through river time.

The land once claimed by the Huguenots, and the Monacans before them, today lies as mostly pasture behind the trees, but these folk seem to have passed on as effortlessly as the river flows. They left no monuments, not even houses, standing along this river, only their bones and other cast off things. Romance and death seem to cohabit easily in this world, especially near a spot called Maiden's Adventure, or Maidens. Here, it is told, a maiden drowned trying to ford the river to aid her lover, set on by scalping Indians as he

Crossing the river on a rope ferry, 1888.— *Valentine Museum*

picked flowers for her. Only the name remains, although the same wild flower probably still blooms each spring. The Monacans did not even leave a romantic story to history before they moved up the river, only the hearthstones and axes exposed by each flood.

As we float past anglers trying to lure smallmouth bass away from their comfortable niches, I try to visualize those restless anadromous species which once reproduced in this clear water. For centuries people above the Falls depended on the annual spring and fall runs of shad, herring, striped bass, and even sturgeon into fresh water, catching the fish as far upstream as Lynchburg. The Indians took full advantage of these seasonal migrations, adjusting the rhythm of their lives to those of the fish.

Later piedmont settlers were often sustained by the runs as they pushed upstream to new lands. At one time, enough fish were harvested above the Fall Line to provide a six-months' supply of protein for those who had the salt. Little did they realize that they were choosing between fish and navigation when a fish dam was rebuilt just above the Fall Line some time after 1780 and before 1823 to divert water into a canal so boats might reach Richmond more easily. Bosher Dam abruptly chopped the fish migration in half, and the shad and herring were restricted to the rocky Falls for their spawning grounds, except for the few who later braved the canal locks. For almost a century, until restocking was begun, there were few fish of any kind to be caught above Bosher Dam. Yet I can find no record of anyone complaining about the drastic impact of the dam; perhaps no one made the connection.

These musings stop abruptly. Bosher Dam, now ten feet high, blocks our progress just as surely as it did that of the shad and the herring. Our float on the river must halt but my float through time continues, in the more sedate world of libraries. The books, though, offer few clues about what the James looked like above the Fall Line before people started reshaping the river and its basin. Those who came to settle refrained from nonessential descriptions and quickly set to their practical activities. But there were some witnesses who did record their impressions who can help me recreate today what the Falls area, at least, must have looked and sounded like at the end of the eighteenth century.

Just before the Revolution, as the new city of Richmond was organizing itself, another John Smyth, John F. D. Smyth to be exact, noted that "the river's cascade hardly felt the restraints of man." He described a "vast current of water" which "rushes down, with an astonishing roar that is heard for many miles distance" between "hills of a great height" which abound "with prodigious rocks and large stones as well as trees." Houses built on these hills had a "wild, grand, and most elegant perspective."

A few years later, a Hessian surgeon named Dr. Johann David Schoepf designated the James as "one of the greatest and most beautiful of American streams." He too remarked on the "foaming uproar," claiming it could be heard at night "not only throughout the town but, before the wind, for several miles around." The scope of the sound of the rapids' roar through the city has contracted today, engulfed by modern noise levels and dampened by construction perhaps. Or is it that no one listens? Be that as it may, the granite sculpture lining the bottom and sides of the river for miles here is not so different two centuries later, though it is more exposed in places because of dams and water use.

The rocks of the Falls are huge chunks of granite, some incorporating the harder and darker xenoliths or "foreign stone," undulating across the river bed, dipping and breaking along fault lines where the water has worn most persistently. Most remarkable are the many deep potholes formed by harder rocks from upstream trapped in a crack and spun by the river. Thoreau described well the making of potholes:

A stone which the current has washed down, meeting with obstacles, revolves as on a pivot where it lies, gradually sinking in the
course of centuries deeper and deeper into the rock, and in new
freshets receiving the aid of fresh stones which are drawn into this
trap and doomed to revolve there for an indefinite period, doing
Sisyphys-like penance for stony sins, until they either wear out, or
else are released by some revolution of nature.

The grinding stones are long gone, but their marks remain.

For a long time, observers speculated that only Indian
hands could have scooped out the hundreds of potholes,
probably to grind corn, for they assumed that human intel-
ligence was required to make such symmetrical depressions.
Very likely there are still those who would like to dispute
the geological explanation, for there is something a bit fear-
ful about the kind of force capable of this carving. Or perhaps it is hard to conceive that the regularly shaped holes
were not made mechanically for some legitimate human use.

The person most identified with both the art and geology
of the Falls at the time is the architect Benjamin Latrobe. He
came to Richmond from Britain in the closing years of the
eighteenth century to design a penitentiary high above the
river. His first impression was that Richmond resembled its
namesake on the Thames, except for "the want of finish and
neatness in the American landscape." Here was "the grandeur of Nature" as opposed to the "perfection of cultivation." The rugged beauty of the rocks particularly intrigued
him and he sketched and wrote extensively in his journal,
exploring explanations for their shape and geologic origins.
But his scientific inquiries did not restrict his aesthetic ap-
preciation. The juxtaposition of rushing water and rock
took center stage in watercolor paintings he did of the
region.

Yet Latrobe was just as fascinated by the possibility of
river improvements that would help eliminate the wild

grandeur he admired. He praised an extensive wooden and stone weir constructed at the lower end of the Falls to direct water into a canal as well as stop the shad and herring on their spring run. He found it "boldly conceived and admirably executed . . . likely to last for many years, if not for centuries." His only complaint about the canals being dug around the Falls was that his own architectural talents were being ignored. Though he took certain pride in not being a Virginian, his ability to mix aesthetic delight in the wild river with practical considerations about taming the James was typical of the contradictory nineteenth-century attitudes about the river expressed by native Virginians.

Latrobe was particularly taken with an 80-acre island in the Falls, the one that William Byrd called Broad Rock, which was then owned by Bushrod Washington and called Washington's Island. Latrobe's enchantment with this island has bequeathed us a detailed portrait of its untamed beauty. Evidently Byrd's attempts to find iron ore there had been well erased by then. According to Latrobe's journal, the island seemed to hang precariously in the midst of roaring cascades:

On the south side of this Island the Channel is filled with immense Masses of Granite, among which the torrent roars with great impetuosity, dividing itself into a thousand separate streams, that wind their way through them tumbling in some places 4 or 5 feet perpendicularly, in other taking a course directly opposite to that of the river till met by some other that rushes again forward. An infinite number of small picturesque groups of rocks, trees and water, present themselves. On the North side several rocky islets, and innumerable broad and bare rocks produce the same effects but in a less degree. The largest Cascade, I have any where observed is at this place. The fall is about 6 feet, it is about 30 feet wide, and the depth at the edge of the fall about 5 feet. . . . The basis of Washington's Island is an immense Pile of Granite, abrupt and bare at the West end, but gradually sloping and covered in most places with Mould on every other side. Towards the East is a fruitful hanging plain of about 15 Acres; skirted round the edge with trees. The West end appears to have formerly with stood many a tremendous Attack from the Western Waters; huge fragments of rock that seem to have been violently torn from the Cliff cover its foot.

Latrobe concluded that this island had met the river's "whole fury"; that "Every appearance on the Island . . . speaks the effect of the torrent."

Soon, though, Latrobe purchased the island to begin his own kind of domestication. He intended, as he wrote a friend, "to live there . . . shutting myself up in my island to devote my hours to litterature, agriculture, friendship, and the education of my children." Either the river no longer appeared so wildly furious to him now, or else his boredom and loneliness had transformed the island into a likely agrarian retreat. Then an invitation arrived from Philadelphia to design the city waterworks, and he left the island for the Virginians to develop.

And develop it they did, starting with Latrobe's notion of farming the flat land. Soon that bit of land became more profitable as a race track. Then a small nail factory was built, with a wooden dam beside it to trap water for power. By 1832 this factory had become the large Old Dominion Iron and Steel Works, sharing the east end of the island with a snuff factory. On the west end, that "immense Pile of Granite" was soon reduced, quarried to pave the streets of Richmond. The hill behind it was covered with company houses and the requisite church and cemetery.

The history of this island reflects the early history of the entire lower Falls area. No longer an insular wilderness paradise, it acquired a new name that still stands: Belle Isle. Ironically, the name is said to be a corruption of Bell's Isle, named after a Scottish tenant. The engineer in Latrobe might very likely have approved of the island's fate, but surely the artist/scientist who had investigated geological history and been inspired by the Falls to paint and write a small book on landscape drawing would have been dismayed. Once tamed to serve human purposes, this island proved to be no paradisiacal retreat.

The reshaping of Belle Isle was gentle in comparison with what was happening to the high ground north of the river at the Fall Line early in the nineteenth century. Byrd, Latrobe, and others describe a multitude of sharp hills— actually many more than the seven that the city liked to advertise—which had been cut and eroded by springs and streams, especially the large Shockoe Creek in the middle of the town which emptied into the eastern end of the Falls. Samuel Mordecai, aged when he wrote *Richmond in By-gone Days*, recalled for his readers in 1860 the contours of that world, with its many hills, gullies, ravines, and swamps. As he wrote, "the city was all hills, valley and deep ravines, and had a most forbidding aspect."

Since much of the sloping land could not be easily developed, there were a number of gardens and park squares scattered about, complete with springs and ponds, frogs, and children. Many springs were left undisturbed since they served as a source of domestic water. Some of the gardens, particularly those bordering the river and later the canal, were minor commercial ventures on the European model where people strolled for a small fee. As Mordecai reminisced, there were many "rural and romantic spots," no longer wild but cultivated to retain their natural charm. However, the pressures of a growing population, especially as the river and canal trade flourished, meant that the luxury of even the cultivated gardens had to go, and the land must be leveled for development. By 1860, Mordecai noted that "the original and the present surface of the city may be compared to the contrast of the waves in a storm, and their subsidence during the calm."

Actually it is most fitting that our lazy float downstream should be blocked by Bosher Dam. It rises as the boundary between two very different worlds, as much today as 3,000 years ago. Upstream is a world where time and men have moved slowly, almost stopping for the past century, and left few marks on the river or its surrounding land. The other world of the Fall Line has been drastically transformed, dating to the days when the dam was raised high enough to remold the river, and only a heroic effort of infusing historical accounts with imagination can begin to restore it. There is little peaceful floating through this world, either through time or the Falls, only the rambunctious interplay of the energies of people and the river they had claimed.

TAMING THE FALLS

THE RIVER'S "roar" was a constant reminder of its flow, strong and continuous. Right at the doorsteps of Richmond was a raw, elemental force which could be harnessed to make the lives of its people richer and more comfortable. Thus it was the inventive imagination, not the artistic, which was challenged to find ways to link people with the river's flow for profit. Born like a mechanical Aphrodite out of the river's juxtaposition of flowing energy from upstream with navigability downstream below the Fall Line, the early stages of the industrial revolution had come to Virginia. The scenic beauty was a bonus, useful perhaps for poets and painters, but far more irresistible was the river's apparent invitation to prosperity and progress.

The river was as temperamental as ever, but with black blasting powder, canals could be cut on both sides of the area to control and sustain the necessary flow. For years the Byrds had successfully operated a canal-fed flour mill on the south side at Manchester, setting the precedent. By the 1790s farmers were growing wheat upstream and transporting it down to the mills in bateaux. The extended James River Canal was an impending reality. Meanwhile the world market was waiting for whatever flour could be shipped on down the James and out the Bay. The stage was set for the rise of the great flour mills on the Fall Line, building on the success of the long-established Byrd mill at Manchester.

The largest mills, the Gallego and Haxall Mills, were thriving, family-run businesses through the nineteenth century. They burned down and were flooded fairly regularly, only to be rebuilt on a larger scale. By mid-century, they were joined by other Falls mills in shipping out their flour to South America and to the San Francisco gold rushers. Gallego had a fleet of three dozen schooners, carrying flour as far as Australia. Until war came, Richmond was considered the flour milling capital of the country, the hemisphere, and perhaps even the world.

The lower miles of the Falls were increasingly lined with mills that briefly captured the force of the flow to coat paper, spin cotton and twine, forge iron, and grind flour. Cotton mills also proliferated at Petersburg, at the Fall Line of the Appomattox. But Virginians were proudest of their iron mills. The need for cannon in the Revolution had initiated this industry at Westham Foundry near the north end of the Falls. The combination of a ready supply of coal from the Midlothian seams nearby, iron ore barged from the mountains, and a steady flow of water guaranteed by canals assured a healthy iron industry. Not incidentally, there were also numerous black slaves who could be more profitably hired out to do work that most white men disdained, for the tidewater tobacco fields were no longer so fertile. Old Dominion Iron and Nail Works on Belle Isle became famed for its horseshoes and nails, but it was a small operation by comparison with the massive Tredegar Iron Works on the northern bank. Tredegar, one of the first strong industrial corporations in the South, grew quickly to meet the increasing world demand for iron, especially for building rails for the railroads. Over the years it also turned out munitions for three wars, the Civil War and both World Wars.

Dunlop Mills, at south end of Mayo's Bridge, Richmond, in 1865. The wooden bridge replaced the bridge burned when the city fell to the Union Army. — *Valentine Museum*

The industries cluttering the river banks meant that the Falls had lost their original claim to spectacular natural scenery. For several miles, factories, mills, docks, and then railroads increasingly hemmed in the river, insinuating soot into its mists which was often "so thick you could cut it with a knife," according to the Richmond newspaper. Apparently no one even bothered to record how the water coming out of the mills and factories looked or smelled. Perhaps the only people close enough to the water to tell found the sweet smell of profit overwhelming.

The roar at the Fall Line had become muted by the "throng of travel, the roaring and whistling of steam, and the rumbling of water-wheels and machinery," as Samuel Mordecai complained in 1860. Canals drained much of the river's flow to keep the gigantic wheels running and the iron cooled as well as to float boats. Even the granite of the surrounding cliffs, especially on the south bank, was being cut back, providing stone for building. The James River Canal, and later the railroad tracks, took full advantage of the land that the river had so patiently graded above the Fall Line. The first settlers' dreams of wealth supported by the river seemed to have finally materialized with apparently negligible costs. The Fall Line wilderness had been tamed to suit people, just as the rest of the American wilderness would be: its original beauty survived only in pale and soundless watercolor landscapes.

A similar story could be told for any major river on the East Coast. Indeed, there are scholars who contend that Americans have never really recovered from the shock of being thrust into the chaos of a wilderness, and that the need to change, to tame and impose a different, more practical, order on nature, lies at the heart of our national character. This urge to "redeem" nature by changing and using it is not just for the sake of short-range economic benefits; psychologically it may run deeper, and probably is not conscious. Rivers in particular can seem like natural enemies, for they may "betray" the trust of people who are dependent on their steady flow by flooding or drying up. They may be neither neat, nor polite, nor generous to their human neighbors.

The thesis is interesting but hard to prove. What is it that compels people to try shaping and controlling the river, regardless of far-reaching consequences and the certainty of floods? The economic reasons usually given seem inadequate, especially when time and events often prove the promised financial bonanza to be limited or illusory. I am reminded that when, as a child, I had a mountain stream to play in, one of the first things I did was to start hauling rocks to build a dam. My frustration when the dam did not retain the water's force for long was more than overcome by the delight of changing the shape and texture of the water for a few minutes and feeling some control over the habitat of the nervous crayfish. I suspect that this determination to shape flowing water according to human will is not exclusively American.

Americans in the nineteenth century were also learning more subtle and ultimately more significant ways to channel their rivers that did not require disturbing the landscape. They literally invited the flow into their own bodies and homes, becoming dependent on its power to cleanse and flush. In effect, they chose to link with the river as new conduits of its flow.

For years people on the freshwater James had drawn ground water for drinking and cleaning from the many springs or crude wells. Wooden pipes were fashioned to carry this water into their homes, but there were constant problems with pressure and quantity, especially for houses on hills. Yet these people lived near a continuously cleansing source of fresh water, purified by sun and oxygen and easy to tap. Logically, then, as a town along the river began growing, to use the river for its water supply made more sense than sinking the more expensive wells.

Richmond males in particular were already accustomed to
the river's capacity for cleaning, for many bathed and swam
in the river in warm weather from the time they were boys.
Not surprisingly, the favored swimming holes were upstream, above Belle Isle and the discharges from factories
and mills. Each hole had its own special delights and hazards marked by its name. These names have a rough poetry
of their own: Snake Hole, Big and Little Feeder, Skin Deep,
Sandy and Gravel Bottom, The Devil's Ball Room and the
Devil's Kitchen, Heaven and Hell, Puss Ricks Chair, Big
and Little Soda Water, Cleopatra, Ring Rock and Big Hole,
and Six Gates. Appropriately, one of those boys swam the
six miles to Warwick in 1820, imitating Lord Byron's feat,
and later became a Byronic poet—Edgar Allan Poe. Most,
though, bathed out of necessity, not as a heroic gesture,
sparing the small amount of tap water for the ladies.

Lynchburg, a town growing upstream below Balcony
Falls, was the first to decide to pump the James into its
homes. To accomplish this feat, the town hired a Prussian
engineer, Albert Stein, to design waterworks. In 1830, when
the pumps, reservoir, and gravity pipe system were completed in the face of widespread skepticism, the entire town
turned out to celebrate the clear water gushing through the
giant pipes.

Richmonders then hired Stein to work the same miracle
for them, for they too wanted "an abundant supply of sweet
and pure water for all purposes." However, a century of
stripping the virgin forests in the river basin meant that each
rainfall carried tons of soil into the river, making it extraordinarily muddy by the time it reached the Fall Line. Stein
had no trouble designing a pumphouse and small reservoir,
but he had less success straining out the mud. He invented
two filtration systems, the first of gravel and sand, and the
second using gravity. These were the first filtration systems
to be built in the country, but neither worked. The prin-

A view of Lynchburg from Amherst Heights, drawn by Edward Beyer
(1855).—*Mariners Museum, Newport News*

ciples were correct, but the size of each system was inadequate to handle the load of sediment then carried by the river.

Soon, though, Richmond, like Scottsville and other upstream towns, had more water, albeit muddy, in the homes. As a history of drinking water in Richmond says, "Then began a parade of righteously indignant citizens who spent the next forty years complaining that their supply was not abundant nor the water sweet and pure." Servants were often required to swish bags of alum to settle out the mud in the family supply, but for seventy-five years little else would be done. Clean public drinking water was considered a luxury, carrying lower priority than building and improving the canal, for example.

All that water going through pipes had to end up somewhere, and that place rather consistently turned out to be the storm water pipe system already in place, sweeping the used water back out into the river. Once, human wastes had been banned from most storm systems—such discharges were a penal offense in London before 1815—especially since "night soil" was far more profitable as fertilizer. But that was not true on the James. As the water closet became more affordable and popular, what came out of those pipes soon put an end to the custom of river bathing. Civic "sanitation" had its paradoxes not generally discussed in polite company. Fortunately, Stein did have the foresight to locate the water intake pipes west of the city and upstream of the discharge conduits. But no one could then envision limits on the river's natural ability to dilute, absorb, and break down the wastes pouring from the pipes, no matter what they were.

So the river's flow became intimately connected and supportive of the lives and activities of those settled beside it. No tobacco leaves were scattered reverently on its surface, for the constant miracles of force and renewal were taken for granted, even appreciated in a distinctly American fashion. And the city most dependent on this river, Richmond, prospered and grew, even as cities on navigable rivers did all over the country. It seemed obvious that Americans had managed to create progressive and profitable cities primarily by appropriating the gift of the forceful flow of their rivers.

Yet that gift was not always free; in any season the James could exact a high price from those dependent on it. Sometimes it almost stopped flowing. Mill wheels halted during the hot harvest months early in the nineteenth century when the drought-dried river only trickled through their races. Thousands of farmers came to the Falls with their grain, camping in line at the two mills which could still capture enough of the flow to turn their wheels. Winter also brought its problems, especially in 1856 when the severe cold froze the river over, closing its length to navigation for eight weeks. There are photographs that show the ice piled high against the one nonrailroad bridge at the Falls, Mayo's bridge; sections were ripped from their moorings.

Sometimes there was too much water too suddenly. With people, businesses, and boats crowding along the James, any significant rise in water level created problems. One "freshet" described by Mordecai is especially dramatic, for it appeared even more suddenly than the 1771 flood had. It was a sunny May morning and the shad were silvering the Falls in their spawning frenzy. Virtually every sizeable rock had its resident fisherman, casting his net into the sluices. In Mordecai's words,

Suddenly, without the slightest previous indication or warning, the river rose so rapidly that all had to run for their lives. Swimming was in a very few places practicable. A great number of the men were partially immersed before they were aware of it, and their access to the shore cut off. As the water rose, the poor fellows might be seen clinging to the rocks, and presently a huge log would be borne along by the current, strike against one of them, break his hold, and perhaps a limb, and sweep him down the rapids against the rocks in his descent. Another more expert would be saved by seizing on a floating tree or log and descend with it to smooth water. The cries and supplications of the distressed victims were drowned by the roaring of the waters.

Spectators crowded the banks on both sides, trying to rescue the hapless fishermen, but twenty men were drowned.

There were other floods of less catastrophic proportions, which regularly washed out buildings, mills, bridges, and wharfs, especially in the valley of Shockoe Creek. For Mordecai, nostalgic for the flowering plain of his youth, there was poetic justice to be found here: "the creek, not reconciled to the encroachment, sometimes rises in its wrath and drives the invaders from their watery regions." But they were not driven far or for long. Low-lying property, because of its proximity to navigation and water power, was both valuable and popular, flood or no flood. Those put out of business by the water were simply replaced by others glad of a bargain.

A more constant barrier to trade than water level was the river itself. Manchester, once a trading center, had lost many of its businesses and merchants to the north side with its busy canals. Although in theory it had the right to half of the water power, in fact it was unable to take much advantage of its privilege. The wealth and power of the commonwealth were concentrated on the other side; poor laborers and freed slaves made up much of the population of what was known as "Dogtown." What was needed was a reliable bridge, not just the unpredictable ferry at Rockett's Landing below the Falls. What was actually built was a rickety toll bridge, a rough affair first devised in 1788 by Colonel Mayo. Constructing a reliable bridge proved beyond Mayo's engineering talents, so the ferry, especially with its cheaper toll, was not threatened for some time.

Mayo's first bridge, only a foot or two above the water and made half of logs spiked to the rocks and half of connected boats, lasted less than three months, or until the next freshet. But profits had been good, so Mayo rebuilt a bit higher and continued to collect his tolls. Benjamin Latrobe, outraged by the six cents toll, described it in 1796 as a "most wretched bridge." At that time, it was still rather jerry-built, of "enclosures of timber filled with loose pieces of Granite," winding across the rocks for almost a mile. For more than two generations the bridge was either being rebuilt or repaired, the victim of poor construction techniques as well as flood, fire, and ice. In fact, it was totally rebuilt at least seven times after encountering nature's fury.

Like any good landmark, Mayo's Bridge had its legend, and no one tells it as well as Mordecai does:

> On one occasion, when the floor of the bridge had been taken up for repair, and the large sleepers remained, the keeper of the toll-gate on the Island was aroused one dark night, and to his astonishment, found not only a man but also a horse waiting to pass. "For God's sake, how did you get here?" he asked. "By the bridge, to be sure! how else should I?" replied Isham Randolph. "No other man could have done it," said the toll-taker; "the floor is taken up." "Well," said Mr. Randolph, "floor or no floor, I rode here, and now I'll pay my toll." "Pass on, Mr. Randolph; I won't take toll from a man who rides where there is no bridge."

Between tolls and repairs, the longstanding division between the residents of both sides of the river was hardly eased by Mayo's bridge which was the only nonrailroad bridge across the rocks for most of the nineteenth century.

There were limits to how effectively people could control or cross their river then, although they kept trying. But they encountered more solid limits when they tried to protect the way of life they had developed along this river, as well as in the South. Dreams of prosperity would be interrupted and changed because another kind of force had come up the river.

PAUSING FOR WAR

SEVERAL MILES downstream from the Fall Line, at the sharp bend where the river begins swinging into loops, is a cliff of clay poised unsteadily above an eroding bank. The iron cannon and wooden platform near its edge are barely visible from the river, obscured by trees that have conquered the trenches and mounds of soil.

I like to squat on the platform, playing lookout and listening to the park tape that recreates the story and sounds of battle. But no matter how intensely I look, there are no ghostly Union invaders coming around the curls—unless barges of gravel and foreign ships loaded with tobacco can count. Not many tourists join me in these woods close by a busy interstate. But for years this spot—known as Drewry's Bluff and now maintained by the National Park Service, marked one of the few decisive victories and a turning point in what was called the War Between the States. Here Virginians showed the world that they knew how to exploit their river's curling ways and topography in war as well as peace. They also demonstrated how apparent victories can prove to be disguised defeat of a kind.

In the spring of 1862 it was clear to Federal strategists
that Richmond was a keystone to victory. Other Southern
cities such as Memphis, Nashville, and New Orleans had
been taken, but now this metropolitan heart of the war machine and the capital of the Confederacy must go. That
seemed to pose little problem, since the Union navy could
back up troops on both the York and the James rivers, so
General McClellan shipped his army to Hampton Roads.
But the entrance to the James was blocked, not by ice this
time but by iron.

The steam frigate, CSS *Virginia* (formerly the USS *Merrimac*), burned but inadequately destroyed by the Northern
navy the previous spring, had been raised by the Confederates, rebuilt, and armored with three inches of iron and a
four-foot iron beak. It was ugly, unwieldy with a 22-foot
draft, but a very effective guardian. On March 8, the *Virginia* slowly steamed out of the Elizabeth River, heading for
the two large wooden warships, the USS *Cumberland* and
the USS *Congress*, which patrolled the mouth of the James
and Hampton Roads. The Union guard was down, and
washing lines hung from the *Cumberland*. It was hard for
the Yankees to believe that a ship which, as Bruce Catton
writes, "looked like a derelict barn adrift on the tide, submerged to the eaves," could pose a serious threat. All day
hundreds of people watched from the shores as the Federal
fire bounced off the *Virginia's* iron plates and both Union
warships burned and sank.

The next day the *Virginia* encountered a far more worthy
opponent, for the recently built USS *Monitor* had arrived at
Hampton Roads in the nick of time. Described as a "tin can
on a shingle" but more maneuverable than the Confederate
ironclad, it challenged the *Virginia*, and they battled to a
draw by noon. For the next two months, the rival ironclads
glared at each other in Hampton Roads, each unwilling to
risk destruction, while Union plans to advance up the James

River were stymied. When finally the Confederate forces had to retreat from Norfolk, the *Virginia*, its draft too deep to navigate the river channel, had to be blown up.

Now the *Monitor* could proceed up the James with its squadron. It was no easy journey as the *Monitor* "inched its way through a narrow and intricate channel for thirty miles in constant fear of torpedoes and fire ships." Sharpshooters along the river picked off men from the decks, but the boats kept moving. At one of the last bends before the river straightens toward Richmond, the channel narrows and moves toward Drewry's Bluff, more than a hundred feet high and towering over the generally flat countryside with unobstructed view at least a mile in each direction. At Fort Darling, seven miles from Richmond, were perched the biggest Confederate guns, looming over a river channel blocked by pilings and sunken boats. Across the river on a lower hill, Chaffin's Bluff, was Fort Harrison; together they constituted a Gibraltar for Richmond.

Against this union of nature and military strategy, even an ironclad could do little. The Federal ships never had a chance at victory in this position, especially since there was no way to raise the *Monitor's* turret guns high enough to hit the cliff fortifications. The inadequately armoured *Galena* took heavy fire and its iron works shattered and wounded many. The Union forces would not capture Richmond by traversing this well-defended river.

General McClellan then moved over land toward the city, only to run into another obstacle course, presented this time by the swampy reaches of the Chickahominy, which joins the James below Jamestown. Without maps or understanding of how to deal with a river which has up to a mile of low land—swamp, marsh, and bog—on each side, McClellan had met an enemy he underrated. The bridges he ordered would do little good if storms raised the river, as they did. One bridge barely held, as did the Union lines, in the ensuing bloody Confederate attack at Seven Pines; the only winner seems to have been the river. The Union forces were still thwarted in their push to Richmond.

Believing that he was greatly outnumbered, General McClellan was reluctant to press on, especially since rain kept falling. Soon General Lee, persistent though his force was small, did force McClellan to retreat back to the James below Richmond where his gunboats waited at Harrison's Landing (Berkeley). Though they could not attack the Federal fleet guarding the landing, the Confederates rejoiced over their victories. In August, Lincoln called McClellan and his army back to north Virginia, despite McClellan's protest that "It is here on the banks of the James that the fate of the Union should be decided."

Then followed two devastating years of war which literally bled the South of men. But it would be spring of 1864 before Federal troops returned in force to the James to try to take Petersburg and Richmond. Meanwhile, Drewry's Bluff was reinforced and the Confederate Naval Academy established there. The curls of the river below the bluff were blocked with mines, most notable the electric torpedoes invented by Matthew Maury. Though the Union had the naval advantage, their ships entered the winding portion of the river at great risk.

In 1863, the USS *Commodore Barney* was spared only because the charge under it was set off prematurely. The gunboat *Commodore Jones* was less fortunate at Deep Bottom a year later, for it was destroyed as it passed over a 2,000-pound electric torpedo. Angry soldiers from the accompanying ships captured the Confederate soldiers who set the charge and wisely tied one to the bow of the forward gunboat. As one historian recounts, "recognizing that the ship's fate would be his own," the man decided to inform and "thereby became a truly animated and effective, albeit unorthodox, minesweeper." Even with this information, a river

"The Ericson Battery Monitor Driving off the Merrimac," from
Harper's Magazine (1862). — *Virginia State Library*

reinforced with explosives was a formidable barrier, especially with its commanding bluff fort.

Meanwhile, inhabitants of Richmond took advantage of their clear portion of the James. For fifty cents, they could take a steamer to the bluff and be entertained with music en route. On a single day in May 1863, 800 people came to watch the midshipmen in their maneuvers and gloat over their river bastion. The James also became the scene of mass baptisms as religious revivals swept the area. The continuing battles must have seemed very remote on these waters protected by the river's topography and man's ingenuity.

Not everyone was free to take such pleasure on the river, however. Libby Prison, high on Church Hill, was overflowing with Union prisoners of war by June 1862, so the enlisted men were separated out and sent to Belle Isle. The Confederates had found another way to use the river's topography, for the rushing waters sweeping around the island enforced its natural boundaries. During the summers, conditions were not too bad for the prisoners; at least there was ample water for drinking and bathing, an advantage the officers on the hill did not have. But winter, especially since as many as 6,000 men were crowded on the four acres of level ground and only two-thirds had the flimsy protection of tents, meant death from exposure. The island was no edenic Belle Isle for the total of 20,000 prisoners who were forced to live there, but rather a kind of human wilderness.

In February 1864, the Federal forces tried another scheme to liberate the thousands of Union prisoners in Richmond. The one-legged Colonel Ulrich Dahlgren was to strike the city with 400 troopers from the west, moving along the unprotected south side of the river above the Fall Line, and then join the 3,000 cavalry soldiers led by General Kilpatrick. The plan was that Richmond forces would be engaged with Kilpatrick's troops, leaving the river open to Dahlgren's liberation.

Nothing worked as planned, however, primarily because

of the river. Dahlgren's men took advantage of their break behind enemy lines to destroy parts of the canal and railroads and freely plunder houses. But they had no boats to cross the James. A slave promised to guide them to a ford, but there could be no crossing since winter rain had swollen the waters. The guide was quickly hanged for the river's treachery. Dahlgren headed northeast, managing to cross the more docile Mattaponi, but by then Kilpatrick had been forced to withdraw his troops. When Confederate soldiers caught up with him, Dahlgren was shot, his body reportedly mutilated and then "lost."

Meanwhile, General "Beast" Butler was planning to take Richmond from the river to the east. In May 1864, he brought an armada up the James, 30,000 soldiers aboard ten miles of ships led by five ironclads. Dropping a division at City Point, where the Appomattox joins the James, Butler landed at Bermuda Hundred at the entrance to the James River curls. Here he entrenched his troops behind a four-mile line stretching from a bend in the Appomattox to the southern point of the largest curl.

A river assault was ruled out when the *Commodore Jones* exploded at Deep Bottom and the *Shawneen* sunk under gunfire that punctured its steam drum at Turkey Bend. Those curls were treacherous. A land attack on Drewry's Bluff was blocked by General Beauregard's forces and Butler's own indecision. After two weeks of struggle to capture the Bluff, Butler withdrew behind his line at Bermuda Hundred, where he was quite effectively "corked" by Beauregard. Surrounded by mined rivers, Butler had trapped himself.

Unable to move, Butler decided to dig out by cutting a canal at Dutch Gap along the line of Dale's 1611 fortifications at the neck of Farrar's Island, thus bypassing the battery at Osborne's and allowing ships to cut off almost seven miles of the mine-laden river. On the first day of 1865, the powder charge which was to open the canal was set, but it misfired and gravel fell back into the ditch. Now exposed to direct fire, Butler's men could not finish the canal; Virginians thus gained most of a canal they had long wanted, and lost a curl to subsequent silting.

The Union forces did hold the river up to City Point, so in June 1864, General Grant moved the Army of the Potomac across the James. His engineers had to construct the longest pontoon bridge in history (2,200 feet) to carry miles of men, wagons, and horses below Westover. Sheridan wrapped up his Shenandoah Valley campaign by marching south to Scottsville, raiding the bustling town and demolishing miles of the canal upon which it depended. Because of flooding and insufficient pontoons, however, he could not cross the river to reinforce Grant at Petersburg since the Confederates had destroyed the only bridge, a covered bridge at Bent Creek. Richmond's downfall would not come from its river approaches.

With the Confederate defeat at Petersburg on April 2, 1865, the government officials in Richmond realized that the city could not be defended and must be evacuated. At City Point, President Lincoln heard the news and prepared to steam up the river. In Richmond, government workers frantically carried records to the Danville train station, while the only traffic bridge, Mayo's, was opened for retreating military forces only. At midnight, against the protests of the mayor, the departing troops destroyed nine gunboats, including the Confederate ironclads, and set afire all major warehouses and the powder magazine. Finally Mayo's bridge and both railroad bridges were burned, and the city left to spreading flames, explosions, and rioting. At 10:00 A.M. on April 3, the city surrendered and the Federal troops began fighting the flames and building a pontoon bridge.

The next day, Lincoln sailed up the James aboard the *River Queen*, maneuvering slowly through a narrow, cleared channel. As the boats kept grounding, Lincoln had to transfer to a barge to make his triumphant entry. He rode through the smoldering city, surrounded by wildly cheering emancipated slaves, but he spent the night in the safety of the *Malvern*, the flagship which had finally navigated the river successfully. Three days later, Lee surrendered to Grant at Appomattox, not far from the James, and within ten days Lincoln would be assassinated after he had sailed back to Washington on the Potomac.

Although most of the sunken ships of war were later salvaged or removed from the channel, the silt of the James still hides its hulks. Occasionally there are those who campaign to raise the remainders of the old ironclads, not to clear the river or to reclaim the metal but to remember a simpler, more vulnerable style of battle when the river's topography was crucial to the outcome of a war. But the river hides its war scars well and the hulks lie deep.

Just as hidden are most of the marks of the furious antebellum industrial activity along the Falls. The economic toll of a protracted war, the burning of Richmond along the river, and a slow reconstruction were particularly devastating to the riverside industry. People no longer had the spirit to do aggressive battle with the river; survival was crucial now.

But with a bit of river bank sleuthing, there are still reminders of those days to be found. A rebuilt Bosher Dam still channels water down several miles of the existing James River Canal, past stone buttresses that were once locks. At the other end of the Falls, the low Manchester dam still detours water into the shorter Manchester Canal. There is one high set of locks, leading to the lower portion of the canal where ships were once built. No canal serves boats or industry now, and there are no more shipyards at the head of the tidewater. Belle Isle reveals nothing about its infamous tenure as a prison camp, and its northern cliffs are reduced to a deep quarry pond. The ruins of Tredegar Iron Works are slowly being restored, and some rocky dams and channels bear testimony of mills that once straddled their races.

Some of the antebellum structures were wiped out by the high floods of 1870 and 1877, just as the canal was, but most were simply torn down to make way for the next wave of prosperity that would come around the turn of the century. For a while, though, the river flowed seaward without being disturbed much by its neighbors, while the defeated South attended to its wounds.

THE SHAPES OF ART

TO SEE THE river as simply the servant of trade, industry, and military strategy is to admit only the noisier part of its nineteenth-century history. There is another, more reflective view, expressed by a few writers and artists who were less than enchanted with the river's pragmatic present. Like many of their compatriots, they spoke wistfully, and sometimes extravagantly, of the values of the fast-vanishing wilderness, naming a nature that was to be found now more in the imagination than in the developing countryside and cities. This was also the age of Emerson and Thoreau, John Muir and John Burroughs, and Mark Twain. On the James, it was the time of less illustrious writers such as William Caruthers, John Esten Cooke, John Pendleton Kennedy, and "Wor Doow," and numerous minor landscape painters who put the James at the center of their works. Most had to look into a past that never was to find a river wild enough to be worthy of their praise.

The conflict between the merits of civilization, especially in its colonial incarnation, and Indian savagery was replayed in many historical romances and poems set on the James. Although the withdrawal and demise of the Indians was unavoidable, Americans, including Virginians, were convinced that the white man's victory had been qualified and perhaps pyrrhic. Time had punctured much of the arrogant colonial confidence in the superiority of civilization, but it was too late to restore the merits of wilderness anywhere except in art. Many of the Virginia works, whether in prose or heroic verse, paint a sentimental portrait of the forest princess, Pocahontas, as a child of the wild river, gradually tainted by the white culture as her murderous kinsmen hover nearby. Hers is a conflict never resolved, presented more as a symbol of irretrievable loss than as fact. Nature, specifically the tidewater James in Virginia literature, stands as the silent center of the clash between civilization and wilderness.

One of the earliest "historical" sagas set on the James is William A. Caruthers' *The Cavalier of Virginia, or the Recluse of Jamestown. An Historical Romance of the Old Dominion*, published in 1832. Although this is the story of a romance between Nathaniel Bacon and Virginia Fairfax (complete with locket evidence of noble birth) set against the colonial defiance emerging against British rule, it also portrays the culmination of the battle between Indians and white men to possess the rich land between the rivers. The river receives the same hyperbolic adjectives as the book's romantic heroes.

The focus is on Jamestown Island, surrounded entirely by the river thinly separating it from an impenetrable wilderness. Indians, bent on murder of course, periodically appear on the opposite river bank; beyond them, hidden in a wild cave, lurks a recluse, an ancient gigantic soldier who is usually accompanied by "ferocious" storms and will emerge to solve the riddle of Bacon's birth. Our hero, Bacon, repeatedly crosses the river (actually, this is probably the Back River portion of the James), once on horseback, "stemming the torrent" as wolves howl in the background to echo his grief over his aborted wedding. He also takes troops up the river to seek Indians to be burned out, pushed back from the rivers. Yet he is loved—and is sympathetic to—Weyano-kee, an Indian maiden taken in by the Fairfaxes and "reclaimed from the happy ignorance of savage, to the more painful knowledge of civilized life." She returns to rule the few remaining Chickahominies, saving Bacon from death at the stake, but she too is doomed. In this book, the James has become the sentimental incarnation of the wilderness, at once a semi-protective boundary and battleground, where "ill-omened birds of night" and "sounds of wolves and beasts of prey" resound, "reverberating from cliff to cliff."

The river in John Esten Cooke's *The Virginia Comedians, or, Old Days in the Old Dominion*, published in 1854, is still wild and even threatening at times, though a century has passed. But it is also a "noble river," offering renewal and delight for those who flee the "noise and bustle" of city life. In a long apostrophe to the James, attributed to the deceased author of a manuscript written in a "rhetorical and enthusiastic style," the reader is asked:

Have you never sought a sensation finer, emotions fresher, than city triumphs and delights—and, leaving for a time your absorbing cares and aspirations, trusted yourself to the current, like a bark, which takes no prescribed course, stops at no stated place, but suffers the wind and the stream to bear whithersoever they will, well knowing that the wind cannot waft it, the tide cannot bear it, where the blue sky will not arch above, the fresh-waving woods will not mirror their tall trunks and fine foliage in the serene surface?

In order to lose himself to find his soul, the nineteenth-century reader is instructed to go in autumn, "when the waters ripple like molten silver agitated by the breath of the Deity," and like the fisherman who drops his paddle, "trusting to Providence to guide his course," and dream "in the broad sunlight of the past and the future." The reader is assured that if he goes to the river, "gliding over the swaying billows of the great stream," he will "see if there is not yet some fresh delight in this our human life—a poetry and romance unstifled in the heart."

The narrative role of the river is only slightly less "poetic." Beatrice, a young British actress who comes with her father's company to eighteenth-century Williamsburg, is in fact "a pure child of the wilderness, in spite of the external claims which an artificial civilization, an inexorable convention, laid to her time and thoughts." A sail on the James brings out her essential free spirit, when she rejoices "like an Indian, once more in his native wilds." To her delight, a storm quickly blows up, but the frail mast breaks and tosses her overboard. Unable to swim, she is rescued by her future lover, none other than a Charles Waters, son of a fisherman.

The river is the scene of a later bloody confrontation between Waters and Champ Effingham, an effete aristocrat so maddened by his passion for Beatrice that he has abducted her into his sailboat. Charles wins the battle but not the fair maiden until she discovers that she too was born a Waters, not the daughter of the stage manager, and thus is free to leave the theater and join her cousin. After they marry, they move far up the river to where it is still wild, beyond the Blue Ridge and beside its curative mineral springs. Effingham finds a more suitable bride, a Lee who lives in a neighboring river mansion. The message seems clear that the river may be the antidote, even the salvation for an "artificial civilization." By implication, that civilization is not so much the one of the 1760s as that of the 1850s.

A similar nostalgia, although tempered by the lighter tone of gentle satire, marks John Pendleton Kennedy's *Swallow Barn*. Set in 1829, this collection of letters from Mark Littleton, New Yorker and summer sojourner at a plantation on the south bank of the James, is not much less restrained in its enthusiasm for the bucolic tidewater setting. Arriving by steamboat, Littleton describes this "terra incognito":

I gazed upon the receding headlands far sternward, and then upon the sedgy banks where the cattle were standing leg-deep in the water to get rid of the flies: and ever and anon, as we followed the sinuosities of the river, some sweeping eminence came into view, and on the crown thereof was seen a plain, many-windowed edifice of brick, with low wings, old, ample and stately, looking over its wide and sun-burnt domain in solitary silence: and there were the piny promontories into whose shade we sometimes glided so close that one might have almost jumped on shore . . . and there were the decayed fences jutting beyond the bank into the water, as if they had come down the hill too fast to stop themselves.

He laughs at his "lady-like rapture" at seeing Jamestown, "with all my effervescence of romance kindled by the renown of the unmatchable Smith." Both punctuation and a sketch are commanded to portray its deserted splendor:

lo! there it was—the buttress of an old steeple, a barren fallow, some melancholy heifers, a blasted pine, and, on its top, a desolate hawk's nest. What a splendid field for the fancy! What a carte blanche for a painter! With how many things might this little spot be filled!

Kennedy does little to fill those "spots," however, because it is not so much the colonial past that intrigues him as the hospitable virtues of a river society already doomed by its feudal customs and strong intransigence to change. Yet he finds much happiness among those who inhabit this picturesque setting.

The plot, such as it is, centers on a legal dispute over a stream boundary line. The "Apple-pie Branch," actually a swamp with a stream emptying into the James, inspired one Edward Hazard around 1750 to build a breastwork dam and flour mill, all in the name of effortless wealth—"this unprofitable tract of waste land would thereupon become the most valuable part of the estate." As the mill wheel began its first turning, Hazard danced gleefully, exclaiming that "this comes of energy and foresight; this shows the use of a man's faculties, my boy." But he knew little about the ways of swampland, and his mill pond emptied in less than two hours, bringing the wheel to a screeching stop, "a prolonged, agonizing, diabolical note that went to the very soul." As a result, a "large, pestilent lake" had been formed which "engendered foul vapors that made the country, in the autumn, very unhealthy." Business dropped off quickly for a mill that could work for less than two hours in wet weather. Nature soon reclaimed her own, sending a flood to sweep away the decaying dam, and the swamp returned to its original unkempt state.

Hazard's son, having learned nothing, decided in 1790 to drain the swamp to plan a meadow. Thus a protracted legal battle was launched over the boundary between the neighbors, though it is admittedly the "pride of conquest" rather than the land which is most at stake. Littleton appreciates the hilarious turnings of the resulting legal quagmire and all ends well, resolved more by good will than law. The "Apple-pie Branch" is left to its own unruly ways.

Unfortunately, the humorous grace that redeems the popular nostalgia of *Swallow Barn* is absent from the river poetry of the time. There were some who indulged in metrical romances of many cantos, usually in blank verse or iambic tetrameter couplets and always in high seriousness, published either privately or in newspapers. Although some were presumably set on the James, most celebrated the Indians, especially Pocahontas, and have mercifully remained obscure and anonymous. One little book is totally devoted to the James, not just its Indian romance, making its author the sole, though an unworthy, candidate for poet laureate of the river.

In 1889, "Wor Doow" of Claremont (a pseudonym for Fred Woodrow, according to the Virginia Historical Society), published in the local newspaper of this little tidewater town a booklet entitled, "The James River, or Rhymes, Legendary and Historical of the Old Powhatan." This collection of poetic effusion and tales celebrates primarily the lower James as a river "distinguished for the magnificent vegetation along its meandering channels, its stately curves and the Arcadian solitudes and repose of its shores," truly the "paradise of the savages." Woodrow's rhetoric rides at full tide in the introductory poem, named "The Old Powhatan."

Majestic stream of ancient days,
And nomads of thy winding ways,
   And fair embowered shore;
Where clings the fragrant flower and weed
To moss of fen and slope of mead
   And many a rugged scaur.

Here savage red with paddle blade,
Propelled his bark from glen to glade,
   To chase the leaping game;
Crouched o'er his fire at eventide
And tuned his reed to dusky bridge
   Aside the reddened flame.

Here bent his bow and shaped his spear
For mortal foe or timid deer,
   And sharped the flinty stone
For peaceful chase, or wild affray,
In forest swamp or distant bay,
   Or gorges grim and lone.

The bittern 'neath the evening star
Kept watch, along the shallow bar,
   For swift and finny prey,
The eagle on the lofty peak,
With blood upon his royal beak,
   Perched waiting for the day.

The antlered stag browzed in the brake,
The heron plashed in lonely lake,
   Hawks circled in the sky;
The mockingbird in bush and tree,
Gave out his magic minstrelsy,
   And heard the plovers cry.

The whip-poor-will, 'neath summer's moon,
Woke up the wild and drowsy loon,
   Among the sedges damp;
The bark of fox came up the glen
And, on the sedge that fring'd the fen,
   The firefly hung his lamp.

The silvery trout came up the creek,
The roving crab of Chesapeake
   Swam 'neath the cypress tree,
And turtle slumbered in the sun,

And, where the deeper channels run,
  Came sturgeon from the sea.

With trailing vine and fronded fern
And thousand flowers in brae and burn,
  And lilies by the spring;
With babbling brook and gladsome note
Of melody and robin's throat
  The hills and valleys ring.

A garden wild of bush and tree
From mountain side to salty sea,
  A warm and golden zone;
A prospect fair, and yet to be
For nations coming o'er the sea,
  The seat of Freedom's throne.

The poet also waxes as eloquently on Jamestown, the three wars, and the story of the phantom ship. Such a glorious past, he assumes, is the foundation for a more glorious future, especially now that the burden of slavery has been lifted and industry set free. He declares that "the South has entered the era of prosperity," and welcomes the fact that "her solitudes are being peopled, her resources developed." The poet of a wilderness river has retired, leaving a "prophet" in his place, anxious to see the time "when the manufacturer will utilize this magnificent waterway, the husbandman fertilize its shore, the tourist gaze on its quiet reposeful scenery" and even the Northern family build "its fairy home on the bluffs of the old historic James." He sees no contradictions in his dreams, as his poem "The Prophet's Dream" makes clear:

Historic James! thy halls and towers
On vineyards red, and myrtle bowers,
  There dawns a brighter day,
Where lonely hill and silent wood
And ruins where thy temples stood,
  Now crumbling to decay,
Shall hear the tramp of coming feet,
Thy fruitfulness and fame to greet,

Thy glory to restore.
Up-raise the spire—rebuild the hall,
Stand up again the fallen wall,
　And beautify thy shore.

Thy solitudes—of homes shall tell,
Thy meadows hear the tinkling bell
　Of many a folded flock;
The hills be crowned with golden grain,
The purpling grape shall climb again,
　The mountain and the rock.

The sail of ship shall snow the stream,
And pennons in the water gleam,
　Of stout and gallant bark;
The hum of industry be heard
To mingle with the song of bird
　And matin of the lark.

And children cradled on the shore,
Re-tell the tales and deeds of yore
　On thy historic wave;
And North and South to country true,
The flag to shield and duty do,
　The busy and the brave.

No wonder these lines never made it beyond the Clare-mont *Herald*. There is little to redeem their poetic cliches, not even very accurate details. Woodrow's talents fell far short of his inspiration, though we can forgive his failure to mention realistic details like industrial development or working boats. But he spoke for many with his embellished optimism that somehow the best of the agrarian and the industrial myths could be combined in accord with the river's historic past.

Not all the literature of the James was formal and rhetorical; there were a few oral legends circulating that cast the spell of the supernatural over the river. One, recorded by Woodrow, tells of a phantom ship which rides the tidewater that is said to be sailed by the restless spirit of a pirate seeking his treasure hidden "in one of the many gorges debouching on the river shore." Then again, it might be the "tormented soul of some arrant skipper who embued his hands in innocent blood and the African traffic."

My favorite tale, elaborated by William Chesterman, hints of future problems. Where the Chickahominy enters the James is a spot still called Dancing Point, long reputed to be haunted. A man, appropriately named Lightfoot, owned a plantation there with a marsh which he wished to drain. The Devil, cast here as a kind of an early advocate for wetland preservation, opposed the scheme, so they agreed to meet for a midnight "trial of dancing" to decide the issue. "Flaming torches and shooting stars rising from the swamp lighted the ground upon which the contest took place." Lightfoot was still dancing at dawn when he discovered his swamp had become a "field, high and dry" but, as it developed, unable to grow grass or herb. Lights are still said to dance at night over the bare area, and "no fox seeks here his prey." The moral is either that no one wins a dispute with the Devil, or do not fool with the delicate balances of the estuary.

Artists were forced to be more honest in their depiction of the river, for it was difficult to paint the Falls area—the favored subject—without including the riverside industries, the canal, a bridge or two, and, hovering above on its Acropolis-like hill, Jefferson's classical Capitol. The earlier landscapes, usually of oil or watercolor, focused primarily on the river from different directions, obscuring details of buildings. As the city grew busier, so did the pictures and prints. There are almost always people in the foreground, perhaps sitting under parasols to enjoy the scenery or busy with cart and horse or fishing net. Two perspectives became most popular: from the west, looking down on the canal from the Hollywood Cemetery hill, or from the south bank, looking at the town. The dimensions and the detail of the river gradually shrink in the pictures, crowded out by looming buildings and hemmed in by bridges and mills. The later prints, often printed in travel books, served to advertise the

Richmond, from Gamble's Hill, by Edward Beyer (1858).—*Virginia State Library*

city's prosperity more than to embellish the art of its river. However, the most popular print was made by Currier and Ives, picturing Richmonders straggling over the Mayo Bridge with the city flaming dramatically behind them at the end of the war.

Not all artists were so enamoured of the development around the river, only the ones whose prints were widely circulated and thus have survived. I have come across a few others—delicate pen-and-ink sketches of people canoeing between the rocks by Auguste Pleé, and watercolors by Lefevre J. Cranstone of a river with no people, only a few picturesque buildings and the moon casting its romantic haze. There are others, perhaps showing the grand tide-water houses shimmering in the calmed water, but these were often anonymous and privately owned, done by some of the young ladies Benjamin Latrobe addressed in his little 1798 essay on landscape painting.

Some American streams were immortalized in the nineteenth century by artists—the Mississippi River by Mark Twain, the Hudson River by Washington Irving and a school of artists, even the sluggish Concord River by Henry David Thoreau. But the James has not yet been adequately captured either in words or art. Its long human history of combining aristocratic longings with materialistic exploitation may have failed to inspire artistic imagination. Its art does, however, epitomize the American longing to keep the best of both the natural and the industrialized worlds, the past and the future, even if reality dictates otherwise.

FROM ENERGY
TO ENTROPY

HIGH ABOVE the Falls, north of Belle Isle on what was once
called Belvidere Hill, towers a statue of Memory, a grieving
woman carved in white marble, protected by walls which
are etched with the names of Virginia's recent war dead.
Her back is turned on the semicircular river plain lying at
the foot of the hill, long an arena where people have acted
out the ways in which they see their river. Here, where
Memory's War Memorial stands open to river breezes, is
my vantage point on two centuries along the Fall Line. I too
am caught in the fluid currents of the past, but what I watch
is a people's vision and revision of their river.

The prints and histories which usually serve as my guides
through time are of little help in recreating this scene in its
wild state. Perhaps the hills circling the plain were once
cliffs, worn down by rains and cut out by streams carrying
the soil down beside the river. Or perhaps the currents and
floods of the river deposited sediment on this flat land.
However it originated, giant, water-loving trees must have
ruled over the rich soil of this natural amphitheater. But

151

since no one realized how drastically it would change, no one felt this river landscape needed recording.

For a moment I borrow the perspective of one G. Cooke, artist, whose aquatint landscape of the 1830s was frequently reproduced with a print engraved by W. J. Bennett. I join the ladies in the right foreground who gaze at the James River Canal curving gracefully at the foot of grassy hills. But I notice that accuracy and proportion have been sacrificed for the artist's vision of pastoral peace. I must strain to find the tiny mills by the river or the Armory beside the canal, and no smoke rises from the Tredegar Iron Works hidden behind the hill. Browsing cattle and trees in the left foreground emphasize rural tranquility; even the boat is pointed downstream. In the background, small buildings clutter the city's hills, shadowed by an enlarged Capitol. Even the river shows little trace of its loud rapids.

Had the artist been willing to peer more closely, he would have had to paint a far busier and noisier world. The plain below actually was cut by two canals—one near the hills, the James River Canal, which both carried boats and tempered hot iron, and one near the river, the Haxall Canal, which channeled water over the wheels of the Haxall flour mill. Here the river has been harnessed by forces less gentle than the artist's brush. Both canals mark the end of the lazy days preferred by Cooke, when the river was perceived as little more than a picturesque, fluid highway. Its powerful visible flow has been acknowledged and set to work.

The scene after the war, in the 1880s, shows no evidences of bucolic peace. It is the day of steam engines, especially of the railroads. Rails made at Tredegar have been laid on the old canal towpath, and the mills will soon burn down for the last time. The water is pushed down Haxall Canal by a low dam stretching across the river; soon it will turn turbines to make the electricity that powers the trolley systems winding around the city's hills. Thermodynamics is fast re-

The steamer *Pocahontas* at Westover, 1890s. — *Valentine Museum*

What the coming of the railroads did: Two views of the river from the
site of Hollywood Cemetery, Richmond. Above is a lithograph from a
painting by George W. Cooke made in 1832–1834. On the opposite
page, a photograph made in the 1930s, with a C&O coal train
winding its way downtown along the canal. — *Valentine Museum*

placing simple mechanical hydropower, as people find new, more dependable ways to harness the river's flow.

What would not show up clearly in this picture are the large culverts opening onto Haxall Canal which carry sewage and runoff water that increases as the population does. This diversion of the water's flow was virtually invisible to the city's residents, although on hot days the stench in the mills and power house must have been overwhelming.

As I flash through another fifty years, I still see Tredegar, growing with each war. By the 1930s, the mill is a memory, and a steel-gated dam crosses the river, paralleling the railroad bridges, to corral even more water into Haxall Canal to satisfy the growing demand for electricity. The island between the canal and the river now bears another power plant, fed by coal transported by the train whose elevated tracks shadow the island. When the water level is very low, the river virtually moves through the canal instead of its natural bed. Meanwhile, deep below the surface, the canal bottom is building up with trash and silt, carrying water warmed by excess heat from riverside machines and generators, and the sewage flow is even more pungent. The rate of entropy is steadily increasing. No one paints the scene now, for few can even see it; their vision is blocked by buildings, railroads, and smoke.

Another fifty years pass, and it is a June day in the present. The plain is bare on most days, except for marks of the past. To the right are the smashed piers of bridges and the gated dam, both reminders of the river's occasional fury, and the island, still edged by the high railroad tracks, is inhabited only by the empty power plants, victims of low oil prices and air pollution standards. Part of the Tredegar ruins are being restored, and today they host an art show of large canvases slashed with bold lines and colors. It is the city's June Jubilee, and scattered over the island are stages, food booths, craftsmen, brightly colored beach umbrellas, and people everywhere. The irresistible draw, though, is the river edge, especially at the finish line of a whitewater race, where the band music is almost drowned by the sound of the rapids. Most of these people are viewing this section of the river for the first time, even though it is right in the heart of the city. If Mother Memory could only lift her head and turn, surely she would have to venture a sad smile, for all is not dead on the river today.

What I see here is a pattern that emerged in the century after the Civil War, one that would seem to preclude any prospect of later celebration. In actuality the war did not initiate the changes in how people saw and used their river. It only removed the last resistance of the agrarian South to the industrial revolution that was based on steam engines, not hydropower. The need for economic reconstruction and progress was imperative, too important to depend on energy sources which were at the mercies of flood, drought, and ice. The railroad was gradually replacing the canals, the water wheels, and even most of the ships. But the river was not yet free to go its own way.

The James had already done the hardest work for the next artery of transportation in its basin, by carving for centuries a steady grade through the hills and mountains. The canal towpath had further smoothed and straightened the path, even though the canal helped delay the actual construction of the railroad along the river. Beginning in 1838, five short railroads terminated in Richmond, but it took the Richmond and Alleghany Railroad, completed in 1880, to restore the east-west traffic interrupted by the war. The line was soon absorbed by the Chesapeake and Ohio Railroad as part of a system beginning at Hampton Roads in the Bay which would reach all points west. This grand scheme, like Washington's great American waterway, was never completed, but Virginia did finally acquire a transportation link with the Ohio and Mississippi rivers, and coal could now be brought from West Virginia to power riverside industries. The James River line had been built just in time, for the upper James River coal mines, like the tidewater tobacco fields before, were almost depleted.

As the turn of the century approached, Richmonders had new plans for tapping the energy of their river. Electric street trolley cars were coming into fashion, and by 1888 Richmond had eight separate lines competing to carry people and three power companies. By 1890 the Richmond Railway and Electric Company bought out the others, and generated power for its station at the end of the Haxall Canal, using hydropower with steam engines for backup. Wheels upon wheels! Several other hydropower/steam plants also operated at the Fall Line, creating electricity, the new energy, primarily for industry.

Ironmaking continued on a large scale, with more than thirty companies at the Fall Line in 1900, turning out everything from nails and railroad rails to steam locomotives and complete lighthouses. The river must have literally boiled at their discharge pipes. Other discharges were mixed in the river also, coming from the fast-growing chemical, fertilizer, paper, and tobacco processing factories.

However, Richmond was gradually losing its industrial and economic monopoly on the James, despite its railroad and river advantages. Upstream, the city of Lynchburg was also a railroad crossroad, and it was closer to the West and the raw materials of industry. Downstream, the little fishing town of Newport News was transformed into a prosperous port and shipbuilding center. Its deep water harbor allowed the larger ocean-going steamships to anchor with ease, without scraping bottom as they would in the shallower river channel upstream. The natural advantages of the Fall Line were finally diminishing.

The residents of the James had discovered a different sort of advantage in a literally deeper dimension of the river: its invisible flow. After many years of inadequate pumps, reservoirs, and filters, there was finally a steady supply of reasonably clean water coming into the cities. Richmond in particular prided itself on its civic sanitation. Residents were encouraged to purchase flush toilets, and then required to connect them with the combined sewer system. Good drainage was considered necessary to promote health, although where the drainage went was rarely considered. More than ever, the river was an asset, but for passive and not active reasons. Whatever drained in, whether through culverts, pipes, or the many streams, either sank, was absorbed, diluted, and purified naturally, or it conveniently moved downstream, out of range of sight and sound. There was no question of treating any of the waste, not even after the technology to do so became available. It would be almost fifty years before any discharges, human or industrial, would be treated or filtered in any way on the James. But polite people simply did not speak of such matters, much less study them.

As early as 1912, there were those who foresaw disturbing consequences in abusing the river's flushing capacity, and they proposed a law forbidding pollution of the James. Industrial interests lobbied effectively, arguing that such measures could not be cost effective. One Virginia legislator even declared publicly that "The rivers of Virginia are the God-given sewers of the State." And indeed they would be.

People never seemed to have had trouble understanding that they could use rivers to move themselves, especially with pushes from wind, currents, tides, and engines, or that they could move water through pipes and canals to serve their needs for drinking, cleansing, or irrigation. But there are many implications of the fact that the river itself is constantly moving which they have not always come to terms with, no matter how obvious these might seem. They see only the river moving in its bed of rock and soil, conveniently transporting the offal of civilization downstream safely out of range. They forget that the same river also flows through their own bodies, homes, factories, lands, and streets, dissolving and connecting, and that every use has entropic byproducts that can degrade the river they depend upon for food and drinking water.

Yet their faith in the river's natural capacity to cleanse wastes and renew itself is not unjustified. What the river does not sweep eventually to ocean depths it dissolves and dilutes, exposes to the degradation processes of sun, oxygen, and bacteria, and may eventually bury under deep layers of silt. But these natural processes of purification and renewal must operate in the unpredictable and slow motion of river time, and not in modern accelerated human time. Rivers cannot always absorb all the waste load they are asked to accept, especially where many people have settled together, not even with help from technology. And on the James, technology has been more the problem than the solution.

The pattern of industrial development and increasing discharges into the river was only enhanced by the two world wars. Weapons of warfare—gunpowder, torpedoes, cannons, ammunition, even the iron which clad the CSS *Virginia*—had long been associated with this river. Arsenals and armories lined its banks along the Fall Line, standing beside iron works and shipyards. That trend eventually moved downstream, to the deeper navigation channel below the junction of the Appomattox with the James. Here, in 1912, the DuPont Company paid $20 an acre for the Hopewell estate, beside the river and away from settlement, to build a small dynamite factory. With the advent of war in Europe two years later, those plans were quickly changed, and a large munitions plant was constructed to produce the gun-cotton needed for high-powered artillery ammunition. The town of Hopewell was thus born, since up to 20,000 employees were needed immediately and DuPont was even willing to build them homes.

When the war ended, DuPont decided to close its Hope-well operation and concentrate on fiber products at an up-river site, but it joined civic leaders in finding replacement industry. First to come was a manufacturer of cellulose, eventually to become the giant Hercules Chemical Company. Its success, coupled with the opportunities for easy shipping and abundant water for cooling and discharge, soon attracted other large chemical firms, especially that which would become the Allied Chemical Company. Meanwhile, near Richmond a company called Experiment Incorporated was built in 1945 to develop the faster, more powerful aircraft weapons and rocket fuels needed after World War II.

Once, it had been the river's energy which captured the imagination and ingenuity of its people. But in the twentieth century, it was machines and chemicals—especially those associated with war—which held the secrets of energy and, presumably, progress. No enemy ships invaded the river during the twentieth-century wars, but in a sense it had indeed been conquered by "friendly" forces. The sustainer of life had become not only the ignominious carrier of human wastes, but its one-way flow passively absorbed much of the entropic discharges of the new industrial forms of energy.

By 1950, sections of the river were not supporting any kind of life at all. As Richmond and Lynchburg kept growing, the life within the river downstream began disappearing, choked by the voracious oxygen hunger of organic sewage pouring through the pipes. Each summer marked the demise of more fish species until the only life in those sections of the river was reported to be a few bright red anaerobic tubeworms buried in the silt. As one study reported, "the benthic life was conspicuous by its absence." At points close to the industrial discharges the river was not only dead but even toxic. Temperatures of over 115 degrees and a pH of 3 were recorded in the 1950s in a mile of river below a single industry which dumped hundreds of pounds of sulphuric acid daily south of Richmond. Another industry in Lynchburg was discarding 220 tons of sulphuric acid each year. Yet few people knew this was happening.

One sunny Saturday, a family decided to put a borrowed boat in the river below Drewry's Bluff. The young wife, who was dying of cancer, wanted to go water skiing once more before she lost her strength. As she skied, her five-year-old son floated in his life-jacket, playing at the edge of the river, until he began begging to stay in the boat because his skin and eyes itched and burned. The next morning, his skin began sloughing off until he had the equivalent of a deep burn over every part of his body which had been in the water. The life jacket disintegrated when it was picked up, and even the bottom of the boat was eaten through in spots. Subsequent infections left the boy badly scarred. The story never reached the newspapers, and no one knows how many other people inadvertently paid dearly for a day of recreation on the James.

There were some official records of the pollution at the time, however. After World War II, Virginia had been one of the first states to create a governmental agency whose sole responsibility was the management of water quality. At the time, though, its first concern was with furnishing cheap water for the rapidly building industry, especially the chemical plants which had been lured to Hopewell. A report from the Division of Water Resources and Power (a telling name!) on the "Chemical Character of Surface Waters of Virginia, 1945–1946" is typical of others done during these years in Virginia and elsewhere. Despite the fact that in many parts of Virginia the rivers were devoid of life because of raw sewage, it is the color of the water which is emphasized in the report. Attention is devoted to those chemicals which could form scale in boilers or otherwise impede industrial uses of water. The picture the report gives is of a stream which is a solution of chemicals and metals that has absolutely no relationship to the life of the river or its people; the primary goal was clearly the maintenance of healthy machinery.

A Baltimore engineering firm, however, had no political or economic motives for minimizing the appalling pollution problem in the James, especially since its 1949 report was a design for instituting a sewage treatment system for Richmond which would have eliminated the combined sewers. Sternly asserting that the golden rule should be applied to river use, the report documented the foul condition of the river caused by the average of 44.7 million gallons of combined raw sewage and industrial wastes flowing from Richmond each day. It declared that "large portions of the James River have become so polluted that the waste is offensive to sight and to smell, so polluted that in some locations not even the coarsest form of fish life can survive during the lower summer flows." A similar situation of deoxygenation is noted downstream of other James River "hot spots"— Covington (on the Jackson River), Lynchburg, DuPont Chemical, and Hopewell. Not even floods could move out the massive deposits of sludge. The newspaperman who lamented in 1949 the conversion of "one of America's proudest rivers into an historic open sewer" was not indulging in hyperbole.

Admittedly hindsight has its advantages, yet one wonders about the priorities of the Virginia Academy of Science when it prepared its study of the James River Basin, published in 1950. This hefty volume, almost half of which is devoted to railroad development, says little about waste disposal, drinking water quality, pollution, or any other areas where the river intimately intersects the lives of people in its basin. It does, however, note the decline of recreation and fish species below cities. There are chapters devoted to the sciences of geology, biology, chemistry, physics, engineering, medicine, but only the geological and biological chapters contain direct references to the river. Instead the history and structure of academic departments in the area's universities and colleges are detailed.

Meanwhile, that same year the State Water Control Board released a study of the Lynchburg section of the James that detailed the pollution caused by sewage and industrial discharges. A pattern of disjunction and fragmentation of river management was evidently in place: scientists in and outside academia were not communicating, and neither group was being heard clearly in the world of local and state politicians who needed to act to clean the river.

It seems strange that the increasingly visible pollution for miles below the two cities on the James was so rarely mentioned in print. Aside from a few watermen no longer able to make a living near Hopewell, most Virginians—like their contemporaries in other parts of the country—simply did not seem to care. Since waterfront industries and railroads, as well as private mansions, generally blocked any public access to the river, it was easy to ignore the problems and transfer any latent loyalty to the historic river, retreating in the summer to other rivers which were cleaner and more accessible. Avoiding the 60–80 miles of polluted river was no big problem. Most people turned their backs, accepting what they called "that filthy river." The elements for potential catastrophe were solidly in place.

THE IDEAL
WATER LEVEL

ONCE AMERICANS had mastered so many ways to take advantage of the flow of their rivers, tightening the bond of dependency, the next task seemed obvious: the water level must be controlled. Any concerns about water quality were answered with the pat phrase—"Dilution is the solution to pollution." Ideally, the river would be kept within reasonable boundaries, neither excessively high nor low but consistently high enough to flush out waste and heat and keep clear a deep navigational channel. However, this ideal was suited to people more than to a river whose dimensions must accommodate whatever rain falls in its basin and the soil it carries. Unable to control the weather, Americans after World War I chose to try modifying the weather's effects, primarily by altering the shape and courses of rivers. It did not seem to matter if some of a river's natural processes had to be tampered with, as long as the river could be forced to behave itself. The possibility of controlling pollution at its sources rather than trying to keep the water level high did not appear feasible at the time.

Since rivers often transgress state boundaries as well as their own beds, the only organization with the expertise, the money, and the political power to do the job of controlling rivers, as a rule, was the U.S. Army Corps of Engineers. Ironically, military engineers appeared to be the most appropriate managers of unruly rivers. For more than fifty years of pork-barrel politics, mostly in peacetime, the Corps has patriotically kept up the struggle with what it has declared to be the "greatest enemy" of American progress, the major rivers. It has applied American ingenuity by constructing dams and canals, channelizing, dredging, in short, doing whatever seems to make rivers more amenable. The spirit of the colonists whose vision of the river was intertwined with their dreams of wealth has thrived in this twentieth-century incarnation, for the Corps repeatedly argues that rivers are the literal bloodstream of the American economy. Thus, no one could seriously question the need to pour tax dollars into projects to keep those rivers within human boundaries. No one did either, until fairly recently.

The best handiwork of the Corps can be seen on the nation's largest rivers, especially the Mississippi and its large tributaries. Here is an array of dams, levees, and other creations of concrete and rock, as well as a fleet of dredging vessels constantly rearranging the silt on the river bottom. The temperamental river that tested Mark Twain's skills as a cub pilot has been leashed, though it is still not quite tamed. There are many who fear that some of the Mississippi's extensive "improvements" may soon backfire, that long-term and unforeseen consequences are capable of becoming short-term terrors. The victor in the continuing battle between the Corps and American rivers has not yet been declared, in spite of the Corps' detailed cost-benefit ratio computations.

The first attempt to tame the James had been part of an earlier military strategy, when General Butler's Yankee engineers attempted to blast through the peninsula at Dutch Gap in 1865. Clearing the loosened dirt out of the cut after the

Looking east from 15th and Main Streets, Richmond, during the 1870 flood. — *Valentine Museum*

war was over was simple enough, and many applauded the convenience of the shorter, straighter navigation route. There have been consequences, though, for the cut-off portion of the river began filling up with silt until the only evidence of the former bend today is a swamp and a "gut" into which heated waters of a coal-fired electric power plant are discharged. Another pattern had been confirmed on the river: first, change the river for human convenience and later, find ways to deal with, even to take advantage of, the unpredicted consequences of those changes.

Although the Corps has had its hand in the reshaping of the James, it has been more a finger than a fist. In the 1930s it continued the straightening process by cutting through two more curls, creating two islands. One subsequently became a wildlife preserve and the other has been mined for its gravel. So far neither curl has silted up, although the swamp area is increasing and it is likely only a matter of time. If a closed curl proves to be a problem (for a sewage treatment plant is scheduled to discharge its effluent into the flow inside one curve), then the Corps will be asked to deal with it also, probably by dredging.

The Corps has become quite skilled at dredging the tidewater James, working constantly to keep at least a 25-foot shipping channel cleared to the ports below the Fall Line. It has not been an easy task; in 1963 the Corps had to build a hydraulic model of the James in Vicksburg, Mississippi, to study the shaping processes peculiar to this river so it can control them better. The James is still not quite tamed, however. Ocean-going ships are allowed to negotiate the river only during daylight hours and under the direction of an experienced pilot, for the channel shifts and builds up faster than the Corps can clear it. A new problem confronts the Corps: the sediments shifted by the dredges are increasingly contaminated by chemicals from industries and land runoff. This one will not be solved so easily as by building a physical model.

Keeping a channel scooped out is a relatively simple though expensive operation. Far more challenging is the responsibility the Corps has assumed for keeping a steady average flow in the river, somewhere between too much and too little. Few people realize how closely keyed most human uses of a river are to its average daily flow. Engineers now calculate how much water will be required to supply cities and irrigate farms, how much to flush and absorb effluent from sewage treatment plants and heat from factories and power plants, how much to float large ships, and how much to turn turbines. In short, they figure how many million gallons a day are constantly needed to support life, both organic and mechanical, in and around the river. Then regulatory agencies can permit almost any amount of development, as long as the total usage requires much less water than the river usually provides. Ordinarily, this system of water allocation works, especially since turbines and ships are not too particular about the quality of water they use.

These averages, though, may reflect some wide and sometimes unpredictable extremes, and therein lies the problem. The average freshwater discharge of the James is 7,500 cubic feet per second, but extremes have been recorded as low as 329 cfs and as high as 325,000 cfs. An unusually heavy rainfall or snow melt in the basin can turn a dependable flow into an outraging torrent in a matter of hours. On the James, this can and does happen in any season in any year. Each generation can count on dealing with three or four "monster" floods with little warning, interspersed with drought lows at least once every three years. Planning is further complicated by the fact that the highest and lowest levels can occur in successive months in this "flashy" river.

Floods usually get the most attention, but low levels of water, predictable by season though not by year, can prove to be more annoying and ultimately more expensive. Reduced water quantity means reduced quality of drinking water, loss of crops dependent on irrigation, stagnation that chokes fish life, and shutdown of industries dependent on great quantities of cooling water. Ironically, the desired increase in flow after rainfall can cause more problems than it solves as storms flush out the sewers of older cities and leach chemicals from farmland.

Calculations for water use are now geared to the lowest levels recorded for the river in a decade to make certain that the minimal flow is clean enough not to endanger human and fish life or corrode machinery. Thus, low water, depleted by drought and heat in the basin, translates into very expensive water treatment facilities which may function at full capacity for only a few weeks in a dry season. Upriver dams may help augment the summer flow, but they too are costly. Every gallon of water drawn from the river when it is at its lowest levels, then, eventually bears an unimaginable price tag.

The Corps began addressing the problem of periodic low flow levels in the James in the early 1950s, planning at least three dams on the upper tributaries which could store water for summer release. This method of "flow augmentation" was their answer to the increasingly visible water quality problems below cities; dilution rather than sewage treatment seemed the cheapest way to reduce the concentration of pollutants. At the time, Richmond had to divert much of the river's summer flows into canals to provide drinking water or produce electricity. What was left in the bared river bed was often largely untreated sewage, which fed thick mats of algae. Similar water quality problems at Lynchburg prompted its newspaper to publish a pamphlet in 1949 on "Cleaning the James" which pinpointed the James' varying streamflow as the chief culprit in water pollution. Evidently, both the Corps and river residents saw logic in operating the river on the principles of a flush toilet.

Only one of those three dams has been built, and that was the result of an extensive campaign by a Chamber of Commerce executive in the upper basin of the James, Benjamin Moomaw. High in the Allegheny mountains, near the West Virginia line, was a deep and wild gorge carved by the Jackson River which had long been a private wildlife preserve. Both Moomaw and the Corps believed that gorge should be dammed. Meanwhile there were many obstacles to be hurdled. Twelve miles of trout stream would be eliminated by the reservoir, as well as countless Indian archaeological sites, but agreements were eventually worked out with the state agencies concerned. Finally the Corps was authorized to build an earthen dam at an estimated cost of $17 million. This became $82 million after extensive caverns were belatedly discovered on one side of the dam. Tons of concrete had to be poured and a monitoring system installed to make certain that the dam would not be undermined. Typically, the Corps chose to try to solve the problems, and did not consider abandoning the project as unwise. Gathwright Dam was completed in 1979 and the reservoir began filling.

Like many Corps projects in the country, this one has proved a mixed blessing, with some empty promises. A number of former Indian sites were hastily surveyed, just enough to see how many would be submerged. There was no time for the detailed studies that could have contributed to archaeological scholarship. The trout population has not fared much better. A new strain of rainbow trout from Nebraska has recently been stocked in the lake in hope that they will spawn upstream. Meanwhile, if they do not survive, the hardier bass, bluegill, and channel catfish which have also been stocked will probably flourish. Thus, the ecological equation of the stream has been changed by the dam. There is still a trout stream below the dam, but landowners there have gone to court to try to keep "outlanders" from wading in their stream. The case may be decided outside of court, however. A proposal to retrofit the dam to produce peak electric power, if accepted, is likely to erode

Aerial view of Gathright Dam, before filling. —*U.S. Army Corps of Engineers*

the stream. Whether the sensitive trout, either the native or the stocked species, can endure all this interference with their habitat remains to be seen.

The argument for flow augmentation once so loudly touted is now rarely mentioned. No one wants to be reminded that the reservoir must be kept relatively low behind that earthen dam, just in case there are more undiscovered caverns. At best, the reservoir can probably contribute little more than a half inch to the water level at the Fall Line. However, dilution has become less crucial now that most of the urban sewage can be treated, not just flushed, and almost no water has to be diverted out of the river bed.

What is currently advertised is the opportunity that Moomaw Lake offers for a tourism bonanza in this remote and economically depressed region. The federal government, however, needs to find another $8 million to build up the recreation potential. I wonder if this is not another chimera. When I visited one weekend in the fall of 1983, at the height of the famed leaf color, the picnic tables and boat docks were deserted. To me, the tall dam looming across the gorge, with water lapping at its foot, looked like an ugly monument to the great American boondoggle and human inability to cope with natural processes. Yet the U.S. Army Corps of Engineers still holds its portfolio of dam projects, and a private organization in the basin keeps pressing for more dams and reservoirs in the mountains. Farmers on the Jackson River below the dam are said to be grateful that their "fences down in the flats" are not "knocked down in the rainy season." Projects like this make me wonder how the Corps can be so confident about its ability to calculate all the costs and benefits.

It is not low but high flows—floods, that is—which most arouse public ire and push the Corps into immediate and drastic actions. After almost forty relatively quiet years, the James, fed by hurricane-spawned rains, had the audacity to rise to and above the so-called hundred-year level twice in three years, in 1969 and 1972. Even though the James floods significantly on the average of once a decade and the floodplains are clearly marked on property deeds, and there were 48 to 72 hours of warning, most river dwellers were unprepared to cope with the generous waters. Few lives were lost in either flood, but the rhythm of life was temporarily disrupted and literally disconnected. Arteries of cross-river traffic were blocked as the waters rose on bridge access roads that dipped into the floodplain and almost 100 low-lying bridges were broken, tearing downstream with a few drowned cows to nudge the quaking supports of other bridges. Potable water supplies stopped after reservoirs and tanks were exhausted and the streams of electricity and sewage halted as treatment and power plants on the banks succumbed to the river. Even the chain of water life was disrupted, as raw sewage and low salinity in the tidewater James destroyed clams and oysters. Losses for business and homes built in the floodplain amounted to millions of dollars.

Up and down the river were angry people ready to agree with Ann Bullington's anthropomorphic description of the flooding James:

Its swirling, boiling waters tear rapidly seaward, motivated by a maliciousness beyond the comprehension of those that know the river best. It is then a vicious thing that throws back its head and laughs wildly at the puny thing that is man, or man made. . . . It is a soulless demon hungry for blood and demanding its pound of flesh.

Newspaper editorials thundered against the malevolent river, demanding federal funding to clean up the damage made by this "act of God," as well as prompt construction of flood walls and dams to keep the river in the channels where it properly belonged. Needless to say, the Corps of Engineers stood ready to lead any battle against the river which had so rudely trespassed on humans and their artifacts.

This time, however, instead of finding an ally like Benjamin Moomaw, the Corps encountered an opponent to its

View of the C&O tracks along the canal, from Huguenot Bridge at Westham, during flood, 1969. — *Valentine Museum.*

post-flood projects. Newton Ancarrow, a Richmond engineer and boatbuilder, had already spent more than a decade campaigning against the pollution of the James and photographing its wildflowers. After the 1972 flood (which had finished off his business), he was appalled to find that the Corps, funded to clean up after the floods, had brought in front-end loaders to strip the river islands and banks of debris, as well as vegetation, trees, and his treasured wildflowers. The next high water would erode many of these islands into the river, Ancarrow knew, so there was no time to waste. As a riparian owner, he could take on the Corps in court. Playing the role of "river nut," using his slides of the damage and conducting a tour of the river, he won his point despite the fifteen lawyers and twenty-four expert witnesses brought in by the Corps and the Justice Department.

The bulldozers were moved away from the Fall Line—but not away from the river. Since federal funding was still available for "emergency repair operations," the Corps moved upstream to begin channelizing the tributaries and the upper James. Here they were more welcome, for residents were still stunned by the 1969 flood that followed 22 inches of rain in one long night. But Ancarrow soon discovered what the Corps was doing, and he understood the environmental damages that could result. This time, since he was not a riparian owner in the area, he could not go to court, so he resorted to the camera, hiring professional photographers to fly over and document how bulldozers were "turning the rivers and streams into drainage ditches." Using thousands of dollars of his own money, he put together a film called "The Raging James: An Essay On Channelization."

In the film, eventually shown twice on the public television station, various experts, standing in front of the scarred riverscape and grinding bulldozers, testify that sections of these rivers have become biologic deserts which harbor little or no life. The machines have loosened millions of tons of soil, sending it downstream to be dredged by the Corps, and stripped off vegetation, thus increasing the probability of drought damage and downstream flooding. Every action taken in the basin is shown to have far-reaching and long-term consequences in the delicate estuary. The point is made that channelization can be a legitimate way to deal with a river, but what was happening on the upper James and its tributaries is judged to be a violent disruption of the river's living processes at an uncalculated cost.

The Corps completed its work and moved on to other projects, and those who saw the film were left to wonder about the wisdom of reshaping a river to control it. There are few ways to measure who won that dispute, and how much, if anything, the river has actually lost. The Corps still has not acknowledged defeat in its battle against the flooding river. Its proposal to build a flood-wall rising thirty feet along the lower banks of the Fall Line and costing more than $90 million is currently making its way through Congressional committees. There is no sense of urgency, for flooding since 1972 has managed to fall within the tolerated limits. But the Corps keeps watch, waiting for the napping dragon to awaken and developing new weapons. Meanwhile the Don Quixote who watched the Corps, Newton Ancarrow, has retired to his home above the Falls.

I too keep an eye on the changing levels of the river, as an apprentice to an art and not as an expert seeking control. The art of riverwatching is rooted in a different concept of what makes an ideal river. It disdains the precise measurements of the mechanical gauges that line the river, preferring a more inclusive and personal tally which measures both watcher and watched. Each day I make my survey as I cross the river's bridges, gauging its height against my private landscape. A small island which bears a tower to direct power lines, a broad expanse of potholed granite, a sandy spit which my toes have explored, a tree which dips over an elephantine rock—these are my favorite markers, but they record more than the level of the water.

Who can explain the strange exultation I feel with each change I note? The low water of summer tempts me to leave my watching post beside the clean water of the upper Falls, and test the depth with my body. I cling to the edges of dry rock, feeling my way into the surprisingly deep and clear currents which wind through the river's center. Here stream the waters which have bubbled from the rocky earth, left by rains of long ago, emerging to sustain the life now visible in the creatures clumped on the undersides of rock or the fish hovering as it spawns. Like the dusty trees, I reach out and a thirst is quenched by the cool, mudless low water.

On most days, though, the river simply fills its channel to its customary edge, holding to the level which balances the many claims humans keep making on it, absorbing and flushing, floating and nourishing. There is comfort and re-assurance in its predicted equilibrium, maybe even dullness. Yet this mean level may be the greatest miracle of all, for it keeps reconciling and modulating hundreds of streams fed by sporadic and scattered rains; somehow the equation re-mains fairly constant.

My pulse quickens most when the river rises, drawing me to its banks where I am sure to meet other riverwatchers. Perhaps the fluid life within us welcomes signs of the river's generous cleansing. As Thoreau said, it may be that "The life in us is like the water in the river; it may rise this year higher than ever it was known to before and flood the uplands—even this may be the eventful year—and drown out all our muskrats." Personally, I am inclined to root for the poor muskrats, frantically swimming as the waters do some forcible housecleaning.

In the spring of 1983 the river stayed in flood, high enough to swirl over the paths along the river bank at Richmond and bar all but the bravest kayackers, but lower than the official panic point. The granite monoliths of the Falls became shadows playing under the smoothed, murky surface. It was hard to find any dry vantage points, so I usually ended up perched on the cover of a high sewage collector. But the show was worth it. The river was busy rearranging itself, right before my eyes, dislodging logs, rocks, and even little trees, and sending them to new homes. There was no way I could predict what would sweep into sight next. I would not have been surprised to see anything, though I was grateful not to see any of the drowned cows or rooftops that bumped down the river in 1972.

Spring was just barely beginning, with the tiny leaves just partly unclenched. Several spots where wildflowers usually flourish in early spring were under water and there might not be any blooms this year. The birds still had nowhere to hide, so they brazenly swooped over the water, pausing on the shortened trees to whistle shrilly, scolding someone—probably me. As the water tugged at the roots of the water-loving trees, scarring their bark with its floating projectiles, I could almost see it rising under the bark, swelling the leaves into life. Just above the water line, on those islands still undrowned, old and new debris was catching the dirt and seed, holding them for sunnier days. Like the four mallards floating backward down the stream, the apparent calm was misleading; all nature was furiously paddling under the surface.

Coming back a month later, when the water was again clear and the rocks were giant stepping stones around the islands, I had to get reoriented. It was still a world of green-gray and brown, punctuated by the yellow and purple of common flowers and the red flash of cardinals, but it was also different. My favorite pile of logs no longer looked like a dragon guarding the rapids. It would take a while for me to find shape here or in the other rearranged stacks, but there should be time before the next flood. The muskrat that lives under the piles seemed unperturbed by the new architecture.

On the river, death by water often translates into new life, and I found almost more life than I could handle. I watched little gray birds with long beaks that I named rock-pipers searching the crevices of new dirt for tasty seeds. On the re-emerged islands were bright green moss sprouting new grass, new varieties of transported wildflowers, and even baby trees. The trunks of trees overhanging the edges were a bit more battered and some had acquired new skirts of rocks and logs, but none looked ready to release its tenuous hold just yet. The flood's legacy of small pools was teeming with life, mostly mosquito larvae, and I scratched in anticipation. Until now, I had not been sure that it was spring.

I have seen some of the destruction wrought by floods and felt sympathy for those who lost so much, wishing they had built higher and tighter. But still, I cannot help but feel somehow purged when I watch the high waters carrying mud and trash down to the sea. I clutch the bridge railing and murmur, "Go to it, old river. Stand up and be counted in this world." At these times even the blindest must admit that the planet and all that abide on it are connected by water, are all channels of the greater River that circulates through sky, sea, and now man. Rivers may not always behave as we would prefer, but their capacity for excesses is part of what allows them to serve other forms of life, and thus be ideal living rivers. By fighting the river's changes rather than adjusting to them, people have eventually found themselves with more serious and unexpected problems, especially when the river defies its so-called controls.

LESSONS OF
THE FLOW

IN THE year 1957 over a million Americans returned to Jamestown to celebrate their river roots. Long deserted, with its banks slowly eroding into the rising river, the island was again brought out of a wild state. Instead of colonial houses, it now boasted a National Park Service visitors center, a restored church, a scenic drive, a working reproduction of the 1608 glasshouse, and a romantic statue of Pocahontas. Nearby a privately owned Festival Park was erected on the river bank, with historical exhibits and replicas of the three tiny ships, the first English fort, and Powhatan's lodge joining the images of the earliest river warfare. Scholars took this occasion to explore colonial history and archaeology in a symposium and in numerous publications. The river's past suddenly took on new life.

This celebration of the dreams and assumptions that had helped shape the river's destiny also marked a crucial turning point in our story, for a long era of taking the river for granted was coming to an end. For three and a half centuries of living with the James, Virginians who paid any attention to the river still saw it as little more than the visible flow of water between two banks, which could be directed and used in many profitable ways, even if it could not always be controlled. Sometimes they were reminded of their dependence on its natural processes, especially when their water supply was disrupted by flood or drought. Public access was still not open on much of this river, which was reputed to be filthy anyhow, so the James had become easy for most people to ignore. What would happen in the next twenty-five years would make people take a closer look at the attitudes toward rivers set down long ago, and to begin to realize that perpetuating those patterns could imperil the health of both the river and its people.

There were unheralded signs that long-term problems were finally being recognized. In 1958, the city of Richmond began operating a primary sewage (or "wastewater") treatment plant on the south bank below the Falls, not very sophisticated or effective but the first such facility on the river. Nearby, Newton Ancarrow had recently settled his business of building fast and luxurious runabout boats. He was already angry about what he was seeing in the river, and he was not one to keep quiet. As he tells it, "All my life I'd been told that the James River was dirty, just stay away from it. I accepted that. I could stand a little mud. I had no damn idea! I was so naive that I would not believe that anybody would do that to a river. I saw times after a rain when the surface of the river was 90 percent floating raw sewage— and smelled it. But I knew it was illegal to discharge sewage into the water, so I assumed it would be cleaned up." As Ancarrow jokes wryly, "They named that river after the wrong king. They should have named it after King John, because it surely is the john river."

Ancarrow might have seemed an unlikely candidate to be a pioneering environmental activist. An engineer, he had spent several years working at Experiment Incorporated downstream, scarcely noticing the careless disposal of

Pollution and beauty.—*Lyn Woodlief*

powerful chemical wastes into the river. Like most Rich-monders, he liked to spend his summers on the river, not the James but the cleaner Rappahannock. But he could not ignore the six inches of raw sewage and thick black oil that coated his boat ramp just before his grand opening, or the fact that boats could be launched only on the few days when the river was relatively clean so that the paint would be neither stained or stripped off. Cleaning the river became his passion, and he took his slide show of sewage and wildflowers (eventually he catalogued 471 species from the James) on the garden club–school circuit, talking to anyone who would listen. He even filed suit with Ralph Nader's Clean Water Campaign, forcing President Nixon to release billions of dollars already appropriated for sewage treatment plants; 17 billion dollars of that went to Virginia. Ironically, many years later the city would condemn his property, claiming that the sewage treatment plant would someday need expanding. The city assigned no value to the boat ramp (appraised at almost half a million dollars), stating that no one "would want to launch a boat in a sewer." But the concern that Ancarrow had aroused—which would be taken up by others who found ways to get to the river—would not be easily silenced.

There were other clues in the 1960s that the bill for centuries of disregard was coming due, but only fishermen and state regulatory agencies noticed them. Numerous fish kills were reported to the State Water Control Board at different points on the river where fish still lived, and the causes were rarely found to be natural. Each year fewer shad and herring, and no sturgeon at all, were making the spawning run. The Commission of Game and Inland Fisheries was kept busy trucking new and tougher fish, especially the smallmouth bass, to restock the river. But fish were not the only wildlife missing. The eagles and ospreys that had once nested along the tidewater river were seen no more. Rachel Carson's revelations in *Silent Spring* came as little surprise to those close to the river, although she did highlight some missing pieces in the puzzle. The river was in trouble, because its ecological links to human activities in its basin had not been seen and acknowledged for more than three centuries.

Meanwhile, the State Water Control Board became stronger as environmental concern grew in the country and state, slowly acquiring the power to demand drastic cutbacks and treatment of industrial and urban wastes. Authorized and funded by the Clean Water Act and the Environmental Protection Agency, the Board could finally act, although within the boundaries of bureaucratic red tape. Fish life began rebounding as the river was gradually freed of some of its burden of pollution so it could begin cleansing itself. But its long history would not be forgotten quickly.

The most shocking revelation of all came in 1975, when the James River became synonymous with one particular manmade chemical—Kepone. For months the dramatic story of this nonbiodegradable pesticide focused national attention on the profound and far-reaching consequences on human health of using rivers as chemical dumps.

Back in the 1950s, the giant Allied Chemical Corporation in Hopewell, that little town which proudly billed itself "The Chemical Capital of the World," patented and began small-scale manufacturing of Kepone, or chlordecone. An organochloride which is quite similar to mirex and cousin to chlordane, aldrin, and dieldrin, Kepone was designed to exterminate the Colorado potato beetle in West Germany, the banana root borer in Central America and Puerto Rico, and fire ants in Louisiana.

But this time the chemists had done too thorough a job. They managed to concoct a chemical which is extraordinarily persistent in the environment, one with large molecules and relatively low water solubility, a half-life too long to be measured, and a propensity to locate in aqueous and lipid solutions. The molecules of Kepone, like those of other synthetic chemicals such as dioxin, are highly toxic to the nervous system of animals which accumulate the molecules in body fat. This characteristic was undoubtedly considered desirable for eliminating fat insects, especially when they inhabited other countries.

From 1966 to 1973, Allied produced 50,000 to 200,000 kilograms of Kepone a year. Its wastes were discharged directly into the James, and no one knew or really cared. Two articles published in 1965 that noted severe physiological and reproductive effects on mice did not slow production or alert any environmental watchdogs. In fact, when Allied contracted with Life Sciences Products, a tiny new company headed by two former employees, to begin synthesizing Allied-supplied raw materials into Kepone, the Environmental Protection Agency declared that no registration was necessary, since undiluted Kepone could be considered a chemical not a pesticide, in spite of its marketing history.

The ironically named Life Sciences company proved to be far less prudent than its parent company when it began producing 3,000 to 6,000 pounds of Kepone daily by operating constantly, day and night. Situated in a converted service station on the highway near the heart of town, the company enforced virtually no safety regulations, assuring its constantly changing workforce that the white powder in the air, on their clothes, even in their lunch area, was harmless. Still no one cared. An EPA air monitoring station 200 yards away from the plant registered 40 percent of the particulates as Kepone, and neighbors of the plant complained to the management about the smells and thick emissions. But in a town dependent on its chemical industries, one where executives' cars can be washed daily as they leave the parking lot, no one reacted. In fact, Hopewell even made an exception to its usual policy and permitted Life Sciences to discharge its wastes directly into the city's sewage system.

Had Life Sciences been more scrupulous about adhering to the safety rules set down by Allied, or had Kepone been a less immediately potent chemical, it is quite probable that contamination of the air and water of Hopewell and the James River could have continued indefinitely. As far as those few local, state, or federal authorities who knew about Kepone were concerned, there was no problem with the chemical, now or later.

As a rule, when a potent chemical dribbles its way into water, whether it be stream or aquifer, and subsequently into the food and the human beings who depend on that food and water, its toxic effects are quite slow and insiduous, difficult to trace and assess. Even extensive scientific studies can do little more than point suspiciously, since firm connections between cause and effect are virtually impossible to establish incontrovertibly, especially when discovered decades after contact. Kepone, though, dramatically broke this rule.

In July 1975, a Hopewell physician, perplexed by the unaccountably severe trembling of a young Life Sciences employee, sent a blood sample to the U.S. Public Health Service Center for Disease Control in Atlanta. At about the same time, the digesters at the local sewage treatment plant inexplicably broke down, forcing untreated sewage into Bailey's Creek and then the James. When the Virginia State Health Department was notified by the Public Health Service that the worker's blood had high levels of Kepone (7.5 parts per million), the pieces began falling into place. Within a week, the plant closed and no Kepone has been legally manufactured in the United States since.

The appropriate governmental agencies now cared. They mobilized, testing the affected people, the neighboring soil, and miles of the river, examining bottom sediments, finfish, and shellfish. On public exhibit were the workers (more than 70) who were verifiably poisoned, especially the 46 who trembled uncontrollably and/or had visual difficulties and high concentrations of abnormal sperm. Tests showed that Kepone had accumulated also in the blood of workers' wives, children, and even their pets, as well as in the many people living near the plant in a low-income housing project and a home for the elderly. Traces of Kepone were found everywhere, from Hopewell's dust to the mud settled in the James all the way to its conjunction with the Chesapeake Bay.

The accumulations of this unnatural ingredient in Virginia's environment were soon found to be far from innocuous, just as the 1965 studies and the workers with the "Kepone shakes" had suggested. New animal studies documented how Kepone could damage the neurological and reproductive systems, the skin, the liver, and the vision. In 1976, a National Cancer Institute report also indicted Kepone in the development of liver cancer in animals. Physicians at the Medical College of Virginia began research to find effective treatment for the poisoned workers, for Kepone was proving difficult to dislodge from the human body.

As the dangers to human health were delineated, the governor closed the river to commercial fishing in December 1975. Also reacting conservatively the next spring, the Food and Drug Administration set the lowest measurable "action levels" on Kepone found in fishlife, saying that any finfish with more than .1 part per million of Kepone in its tissues would be considered hazardous for humans eating the fish. A year later the level was raised to .3 ppm (.4 for crabs) where it still stands amid annual debate. However, for years many fish in the estuary had accumulated more than double the higher level. Around 1981 fishing was again permitted for eels, oysters, and migratory fish that can flush themselves of Kepone, restricting only a few species for the last six months of the year when the Kepone accumulates to high levels in their tissues.

With its usual hyperbole, the media called Kepone the environmental tragedy of the decade, if not the century. Perhaps it would be fairer to say that Kepone was one of the first chemicals to have such a dramatic and thoroughly publicized impact on human health and the environment in this country. Most Virginians, though they love their history, would gladly relinquish the infamy of this particular honor. For a long time, many Americans refused to buy seafood originating in Virginia, pushing hundreds of watermen into bankruptcy including those along the closed James. Paranoia reached a new high, especially among the victims and their neighbors in Hopewell. Suits totalling more than 200 million dollars were filed by victims and watermen against Allied Chemical and former Life Sciences executives. The once-proud name of the James had been sullied among those who never knew her as well as those who loved her. Most people were assured that nothing good could ever come from this disaster.

Clean-up of this pervasive and persisting chemical turned out to be costly and difficult, even impossible in many instances. Kepone residues in the plant and the surrounding soils were trucked out under vigilant control and eventually buried in a salt mine in West Germany. The Corps had to abandon dredging of the James for several years in the area, meanwhile searching for safe technology to use when the sediments accumulating in the shipping channel would have to be removed. Most of the Kepone had to stay in the river bottom and in the fishlife, slowly moving up the food chain, where it was inaccessible. But the "muddy ol' Jeems" has kept on rolling by, laying down its load of upriver soil (as much as several inches a year, according to some authorities) over the Kepone-tainted sediments, thus keeping much of the chemical from being released into the water and its life.

Repercussions from Kepone may currently be more positive than negative, for a hard lesson about ecological connections and chemical persistence has been taught. No industry in Virginia, particularly if situated anywhere close to the James, would be foolish enough to risk endangering its reputation and profits by discharging pollutants which could be toxic, even if the now-stricter State Water Control Board would allow it. They are checked not so much by law as by the awareness that Allied Chemical was punished severely, losing millions of dollars for its role in the production of Kepone as well as substantial public confidence. A federal judge fined Allied 13.2 million dollars, directing that 8 million dollars go to establish an independent grant-awarding organization. Thus the Virginia Environmental Endowment, which supports environmental quality studies in the state, became the first such private organization in the country. Oddly enough, then, because of Kepone Virginia finds itself today as a sort of leader in river management and environmental concern.

Other human benefits are not so easy to weigh, though they exist. Researchers have found that the drug cholestyramine will eliminate Kepone from the human system, so the Life Sciences workers now show few if any physical effects of their ordeal. Some have even fathered healthy children recently. But levels of debilitating anxiety are much harder to measure. Even the level of Kepone in the sludge stored in a lagoon at the sewage treatment plant in Hopewell has been dropping, suggesting that something, possibly the resident fungus *Aspergillus*, can degrade the chemical into weaker compounds. The treatment plant itself has been greatly upgraded, so much that in 1983 the Lower James River Association bestowed its "Friend of the River Award" on the operation. Although people now buy Virginia seafood with confidence and fishing of many species has been allowed recently, five years of fishing bans have devastated the occupation of many commercial watermen on the James. And there are people who still consider the James little more than an obscenity. Yet even that may have merit if it helps assure that people will not forget how easily a river may be poisoned.

The river has offered many other lessons, but fortunately none have been as shocking as the Kepone discovery was.

After the Kepone disaster, lower James River. — *Richmond Newspapers*

Gradually people have been finding themselves intimately linked to the river's flow, and sometimes in unexpected fashions. In a few hours on a sunny September day in 1981, the river turned bright green for almost fifty miles between Richmond and Scottsville, literally blooming with blue-green algae. Powered by the warmth of a brilliant Indian summer and low water full of nutrients donated by fertilized fields upstream, a little organism called *Nodularia harveyana* (whose proper place is usually under microscopes in biology classrooms) suddenly flourished. As algae go, this type was a comparatively innocent one which released odors as it died but no toxins, but it never had bloomed so vigorously in the James before.

Throughout the city of Richmond, the overwhelming and somewhat nauseating smell of wet earth came pouring out of spigots. The odor was ubiquitous, rising from sinks and bathrooms, salads and coffee pots. Though the city utilities department did receive telephone calls from European-bred people commenting nostalgically on the new "body" of the water, most people were disgusted, angry, and suddenly aware of how intimately connected their daily lives were with the river that ran through the city.

Thousands of dollars were spent as officials added tons of activated charcoal to water filters and chemists tested day and night. Newspaper articles about the few springs still open in the city brought long lines of people waiting patiently with jugs well into the morning hours, while stores rush-ordered bottled water for their anxious customers. Numerous solutions were suggested and rejected, including the possibility of using chemicals that would "kill everything in the river." The dying algae backed up behind the low dams of Richmond in what had become stagnant ponds, though some relief came by diverting water into the old canal with its intake pipes to the purification plant.

In a few weeks, rain and cold weather cleared the water, the fish resumed their normal eating habits, and the river no longer imposed its bloom of living and dying algae cells on the people dependent on its waters. So passed a relatively painless lesson that the river has human channels too.

There can also be a humorous side to the difficulties people have had in coping with the incessent motion of their rivers. The problem that the Virginia Power and Electric Company (VEPCO) encountered at its nuclear plant across the river from Jamestown is a good example of how people think "stop" when the river says "go." When the plant began operation, its screens for filtering the water were constantly clogged by countless numbers of tiny creatures in this nursery wetlands. VEPCO had to do something quickly, for it needed the water for cooling and it was committed to minimal environmental impact, but there were few precedents for solving this particular impingement problem.

VEPCO biologists and engineers began experimenting, trying to find a way to divert the fish. First they installed air machines in the canal to blow dense curtains of bubbles, but the fish swam right through, drawn rather than deterred by the oxygenated water. Next, they tried a sound barrier, installing a number of underwater speakers in front of intake pumps. No matter what they played through the speakers— MUSAK, hard rock, classical music, or just loud noise— the fish kept dancing up the canal to meet their doom on the fixed screens.

Finally human ingenuity triumphed. J. D. Ristroph, director of VEPCO's Environmental Services Department, designed a new kind of travelling screen with 47 screen panels which rotate continuously. Rather than blocking the young fish, the screens carry them for a brief ride, then drop them into a sluice trough that carries them safely downstream and far offshore, safely out of harm. It was a clever idea and it has worked well, with a 4–6 percent mortality rate instead of the earlier 95 percent, and the design has been adopted by power plants all over the world.

Unfortunately, simple engineering devices or waiting for
nature's repairs will not solve all the problems encountered
by living creatures in this river, especially if they happen to
live downstream from people who continue to use the river
thoughtlessly. This conclusion was recently underscored,
both dramatically and scientifically, with the publication of
the Environmental Protection Agency's extensive studies of
the body of water captive at the foot of the James, the
Chesapeake Bay. Even the most cautious scientists now declare that the less hardy but valuable life in the Bay—such
as striped bass, oysters, blue crabs, and anadromous fish—is
dying off, and the Bay's system of rivers must assume most
of the blame, especially the Susquehanna, the Potomac,
and the James. Each carries nitrogen and phosphorus from
land run-off and sewage treatment, as well as metals and organic chemical compounds which have seriously disrupted
the ecosystems of the Bay. Some signs may be found right
in the mouth of the James. Submerged aquatic vegetation
which once hid and supported baby crabs and other nursery
animals disappeared here, as in much of the Bay, in the
1970s, victim of overfertilization from upstream fields and
sewage treatment effluent.

The James River oyster is in serious trouble. This tena-
cious shelled creature, lauded by John Smith as huge and
abundant, has long selected the mouth of the James as breed-
ing grounds and nursery. Stuck on its bed, it has tolerated
and absorbed whatever has come downstream, purging itself as much as possible. Watermen long ago learned that
they would have to move the baby oysters to other rivers
and the Bay so they could grow and cleanse themselves better than they could in the James. But the numbers of "brood
stock" and "spat set" have declined drastically since 1960, in
effect undermining the long-established oyster industry of
the Bay. The MSX virus and the oyster drill have appeared,
weakening and killing susceptible oysters. Scientists now
suspect that they may be vulnerable because of chlorine and

other "debilitating contaminants" and increased silt loaded with pesticides, Kepone, and heavy metals, all of which interact with salinity and water-level changes. One study discovered 94 different organic compounds, including Kepone, in oysters taken from the river. There seems to be no question that when the lower river is in trouble, so are the reproductive cycles of the oyster and other forms of life in the Bay.

The lowly seed oyster has thus become one living barometer of the dangers of upstream pollution. Its message—that the entire river system must be seen, understood, and managed with care—is heard all the more clearly because a profitable industry is at stake. The oyster will be watched carefully as federal and state governments embark on an expensive and complicated campaign to clean up the rivers to save the life of the Bay.

The findings of the landmark (or rivermark?) Chesapeake Bay study were first published in September 1982. There were no festivities planned, not even much publicity for a while, and the news was received soberly. Yet there could not have been a more appropriate way to celebrate the 375th anniversary of the white man's first settlement on the James. The modern language of authority, the scientists' statistics, had declared the life of the Bay to be in peril, perhaps dying, and pointed fingers of blame upstream, up the Bay's rivers. Now it was time for people to revise their ideas about the river, time to name it again. To save the Bay, and perhaps ultimately themselves, they would have to go beyond seeing the river as a highway for ships, as a flow to be regulated and channelized to flush through machines, homes, and themselves, and as a ready source of commercial food. Its continuing wealth would depend on how clearly they could see the greater River of stream, river, and Bay, of sea and rainfall, as a living, moving ecosystem, and acknowledge its intimate connection with their own well-being.

SIGNS OF LIFE

THE WORD is finally out—there is life in the James River, and plenty of it. Finding it can be another matter. This is one muddy river, especially after a rainfall sweeps down the farmers' good topsoil and fertilizers. But even at its clearest, most of its life stays hidden, visible mainly to biologists and fishermen who can name what they see. Fortunately for me, they are tolerant souls as a rule, who welcome questions from inquisitive river prowlers.

It is easiest to see the creatures that hover near the water's surface. I need only to sit on a shady rock at the edge of the Falls when the water is low and clear and use polarized glasses to penetrate the streaks of light playing on the submerged rocks. Millions of tiny flies swarm in a mating frenzy where the water is swirling slowly. Bits of blue and green scattered through the black cloud are dragonflies, feeding and dipping their tails. Occasionally, farther out where the current picks up, a smallmouth bass breaks into the air to snap up a dragonfly who dipped once too often. Overhead, a kingfisher keeps swooping over the water, his raucous calls intended to drive me away from his moving lunch cart. Standing near the water grasses with their delicate lavender flowers is a fisherman, casting for bass. I note that "Eat and be eaten" is a law of the river as well as the jungle. But most of the carnage is invisible and distant, little battles in the mud and grass and between rocks.

The fisherman shows me a concrete interceptor sewer line that makes a convenient underwater sidewalk up the river. By focusing on the minnows and tadpoles darting at the edge, my eyes slowly adjust until I am ready to go find bigger game. As I shuffle through the current, a long ugly gar sweeps fearlessly past my feet; he and his kind have probably been here for centuries, but like other inedible or "non-game" fish, they are rarely noted officially. I watch with the fisherman for the colorful sunfish, brim, and small-mouth bass to be tempted with his hook, but most seem intent on more promising food than his bait. I turn over rocks, looking for the larvae of mayflies and caddisfly cases, sure signs of a clean river, but either they are not here or I do not yet know where and how to look. I am, after all, still an apprentice at this.

The fish which now rules the freshwater James, after being stocked almost a century ago, is the feisty small-mouth bass. Fishermen are said to come from all over the country to hunt this fish down. My guide into this select company was a certified philosopher, a colleague whose quest for truth somehow includes searching for citation bass. One summer day we went upstream, to western Goochland County, to float-fish where there is comparatively little bottom silt and the water is clear. We cheated a bit, putting a small electric motor on the canoe to leave our hands free. But that was the only place we cut corners, for this philosopher is a purist who considers flycasting from a moving canoe the only sporting way to take a fish.

First I was carefully instructed about the psychology of smallmouth bass. One must assume that they are as lazy as most people are, and so will bite only if the lure is danced right in front or above them. Rarely moving far from the hole they have staked as their territory, they will strike—at the right kind of lure in the right spot—only once. Often they avoid the hook's dig, and they will not make the same mistake twice, so the fisherman might as well move on, casting again into another place where a bass might wait, suspended against the current.

The theory was validated by practice, because we found some of those bass; even this novice pulled in two. Many more struck than we were able to hook, and some fought their way free. Most that we did catch we sent back home to grow up some more, but two measured more than the regulation twelve inches. My guide complained that it was a slow, rather unproductive day, nothing like the cooler autumn would be, but I was content. After an hour or two of getting tangled in my line, I began to get the knack of casting. By then, though, I had discovered that I preferred to try to penetrate the reflecting water by looking, not fishing. Trying to visualize the underworld that my fisherman friend could see was far more appealing than catching fish that would have to be cleaned and eaten.

It is tempting to keep on floating in this clear water, but I know that it is the lower James estuary, along the river's curving and ragged low edges, where I must go to find the heart of the river's life. Armed with canoe and boots, I poke into the patches of marshes and swamps, the "wetlands" which stretch along the river banks and the tidal creeks. The water, briny in varying concentrations, is a nursery not only for the river but, to some extent, for the Chesapeake Bay and even the Atlantic. In the deep mud and dark waters around the tough grasses of the marshes, which grow on a thick rotting biomass, is the abundant life at the base of the food chain which eats the fast-decaying bits of grass and roots and the algae. This life, often microscopic in size, in turn feeds the tiniest nursery animals spawned in the river that cling to my dipping net. In nature, life often comes out of much death.

Wetlands are not a very pleasant place to be. I sink deeply into the pungent muds, hanging on to their hardy grasses, and the canoe tips easily as I maneuver around the sharp bends of the creeks, startling tiny crabs and frogs. Insects, especially mosquitoes and hard-biting horse flies, seem bent on torment, no matter what the season. But with luck I see the great blue herons, ospreys, and even the eagle circling and feeding on this soggy, rich land. The marsh waters may be too dark for me to detect much of their resident life, but the sharper-eyed birds have no trouble spotting their prey.

Not long ago, say fifteen years, expeditions to the river like these were difficult if not impossible to take. There were simply few ways to reach the river bank legally anywhere along its length. Fences and "No Trespassing" signs were the rule. The riparian doctrine of English common law governs water rights in this state, meaning that riparian owners are presumed to have the only legal rights to use a natural watercourse unless it is navigable; and even then they can prevent access to the river. Above the Fall Line, those owning land on the riverbank can claim ownership to the river bottom and islands, right to the middle of the water. The few who can produce deeds traceable to the original royal grants dating before the eighteenth century— and they do exist—can also legally claim the non-navigable stretches of river bordered by their land and the life within it, including the "royal fishes" if they should happen to appear. By tradition, then, Virginia's title of "commonwealth" has not extended to its rivers.

Since most of the river's banks after the canal closed were owned by large landowners, local government, lumber companies, or the railroad, very few ordinary people could use the river, even stroll its banks, for years. A dedicated nature-lover like Newton Ancarrow (who was also a riparian owner) could get permission to prowl around the river with his camera to take pictures of wildflowers, but not many others tried, or even knew that the river might be worth the trouble. There were always a few boys who found their way, legally or not, especially poor ones with little else to do in the summer. I met one of the Virginian Huck Finns on my first trip to the river a decade ago, when he floated up in an inner tube. His skinny browned arms and legs were covered with scars, each with a graphic tale of an encounter with barbed wire, granite, and impetuous currents he was anxious to tell. But most people have not had his daring, for they are bred to respect property rights.

Ironically, it was a decision to put a highway along the river that led to the opening of recreational access along the Fall Line. In 1966, a housewife saw a dramatic picture of the river near her home in the Richmond newspaper. Superimposed on an aerial photograph of the river above Williams Dam, flamboyant in its bright autumn colors, was a four-mile, four-lane parkway hanging over the southern bank, with footbridges leading from a median parking lot to the two islands. The headline read, "Expressway Opens Recreation Vista." Her name was Louise Burke, and the Richmond Metropolitan Authority had just met its match. She soon discovered that the narrow floodplain in front of the bluffs along the river would have to be built up with tons of fill dirt from the islands. Following the granting of federal funds, the toll highway would be constructed ten feet above the so-called "value-less" floodplain, blocking off one of the few stretches of river in the city, or on the entire river, which was unofficially open for public recreation.

That highway was never built, for Mrs. Burke soon enlisted help from her neighbors, including R. B. Young, a medical school professor. In 1970 they organized the Richmond Scenic James Council, becoming one of the first citizen groups to "adopt" the river. They lobbied effectively for increased public access and better water use planning, not just in the city but with state legislators. At their urging the Virginia General Assembly declared the Falls from Belle Isle to the western end of the Fall Line in 1972 as a "historic

The falls of the James, today. Belle Isle is in the center. The ruins are of several railroad bridges.—*Lyn Woodlief*

river with noteworthy scenic and ecological qualities," thus establishing a Falls of the James Committee under Dr. Young to advise on decisions affecting the part of the river running through the city. It took another twelve years, but finally the Assembly finished what it had started, officially designating the Falls as a "scenic river," giving it added protection and a federal name. Soon the "historic" portion of the tidewater James is likely to be awarded the same designation because of the efforts of another group of riparian owners. People have rediscovered the pleasures of their river, and few politicians would dare question their mandate to declare it scenic.

Today, then, much of the life visible on the river is in human form, especially in the James River Park which stretches over 480 acres of riverbank and islands in six locations along the Fall Line. High walkways span the railroad tracks and canal, descending into what is left of a river wilderness. Upstream, the Audubon Society has dug out a wetlands area which attracts both birds and birdwatchers. Along the river, twelve access areas with parking and boat landings have been opened by the Virginia Commission of Game and Inland Fisheries with more scheduled for development. There are a few other privately owned places open to knowledgeable canoers and fishermen. Recently the Forest Service opened three primitive float-in campsites below Buchanan on a favorite float section of the upper James. There is even a state park in Surry County, but none yet on the piedmont or upper James. The James is now one of the state's more accessible rivers. In spite of what has been trashed or flushed into these waters for centuries, the river species called *Homo sapiens* is flourishing, especially in warm weather, indulging in swimming and wading, boating and fishing, or just rock-sitting.

Public access has brought its problems. Part of the tidewater James can be dangerously crowded with boats on weekends, and aluminum cans and bottles often mark the trails of careless boaters through clearer waters. Broken glass threatens waders in James River Park, and each summer several people drown when they miscalculate the power of the river's current. The familiarity that leads to seeing and perhaps caring for the river has not always bred respect. Some people—and Ancarrow is one—want to see the river closed again and allowed to return to as wild a condition as possible. But people have already left their marks, and they intend to continue enjoying the river they have recently rediscovered.

Recently the city of Richmond debated closing much of the access to the river at the Fall Line because of the expenses the fire department has incurred trying to rescue people, alive and dead, who have underestimated the power of the Class IV to VI rapids, particularly at high water. A group of experienced canoeists began working with the naturalist of the James River Park to figure out a solution to the problem before one was forced on them. They had signs painted and erected at each launching site that detailed the river's hazards, stating that river users must wear life-jackets when the river is over five feet high. Only canoers with whitewater experience can now legally shoot the rapids when the river is over nine feet. Depths are regularly marked, and the level of the river has become a regular feature on evening television weathercasts. The organization teaches whitewater techniques and polices the river during public whitewater races. In turn, the city assesses fines on people who have to be rescued. The compromise seems to be working, and the fire department has not had as many excuses to go to the river lately.

Not all conflicts about who can use the river have been so well reconciled, however, especially in times when cost-benefit ratios govern decisions about water, and those decisions are usually made in the many political jurisdictions through which the river runs. There, planning often becomes a game of determining "who gets what part of the

Aerial view of Allied Chemical plant at Hopewell.
—*Richmond Newspapers*

river." Even when a group with a financial interest in using the river is willing to listen to the claims of other interests, one kind of use often endangers or eliminates others. It is both difficult and expensive to reconcile dams with rafting and fish migrations or waste disposal with swimming, fishing, and drinking the water. Relatively innocuous river pleasures like swimming, fishing, boating, and watching do not seem to pay off in dollars, yet they can require millions of dollars, especially in heavily populated areas of the river basin, to keep the water clean enough.

For every form of wildlife visible in and around the river, biologists say, there is a complicated, sensitive, and usually hidden support system made up of multitudes of tiny creatures essential to the food chain. Likewise, for every way that people have found to use and enjoy a river, there must be a backup network, perhaps equally complicated, vulnerable, and invisible to most. These are the people—bureaucrats, planners, legislators, local supervisors, sanitary engineers, fish wardens, environmentalists, and more—who see to it that the river is allowed to renew itself, that it is kept clean and oxygenated enough to support all types of life. The canoeing dispute is but a small example of what must happen to protect both the river and the people who use it.

On the James there are at least a hundred different organizations, from citizen groups to governmental agencies, making decisions and enforcing regulations that govern the river's health, not to mention the supervisory boards of every county and city the river borders or runs through. They often delay, argue, gap and overlap, for they are loyal to their own territory, their own different ways of seeing the river. Still, the management goal of "fishable, swimmable waters," as phrased by the Environmental Protection Agency and measured by sophisticated laboratory tests and national standards, is gradually, although painfully, being realized on this river. Many Americans will settle for no less.

LOOKING UPSTREAM

THE PAST of a river catches up with the future at its mouth, where its waters and sediments flow. On the James that means Hampton Roads, where the James widens over acres of oyster beds into the Chesapeake Bay. Here the scope of water and the marks of man dwarf one person in a canoe. So in May 1984, I found myself cruising Hampton Roads in the company of a hundred people—mostly local planners and supervisors from upriver and environmentalists—attending a conference on the Bay. All day various experts took the microphone to point out not only what we were seeing, but how the life of the Bay has been threatened by the ways people have seen and used their rivers.

Our boat left from a seafood processing plant where the owner, a waterman whose ancestors fished the James and the Bay, recalled the time when water life was rich enough to support thousands of people. In his words I kept hearing echoes of the ecstatic descriptions of early settlers—of John Smith, Gabriel Archer, and William Byrd, at once listing and praising the water's fertility and calculating its potential market value. Unlike his predecessors, this waterman must range far, to both oceans and the Gulf of Mexico, to find enough seafood to sell to make a living. Reluctantly he admitted that overfishing, not just pollution, has helped deplete the resource, and that only federal regulation has the power to sólve many of the Bay's problems.

We did not have to go far to find reminders of another part of the river's heritage—battle and conquest. Dodging tankers and Navy ships, we passed over the site where the ironclads clashed and one was sunk. Docked at the Norfolk Naval Base and flanked by carriers, battleships, and a growing fleet of nuclear submarines, we heard an officer detail the Navy's current campaign to make certain that its operations do little to harm the nonaligned waters which bear its ships. The legacy of neglect remains, however, up the nearby Elizabeth River, whose bottom is coated with the black creosote, oils, and other chemicals from industry and shipbuilding, and whose surviving fish suffer tumors and fin rot.

Beyond the ships loomed the Virginia headquarters of America's water engineers, the same U.S. Corps of Engineers that has waged so many battles with the James. Ironically its neighbor is the American center of Jacques Cousteau, a Frenchman who fights battles of quite another sort to dramatize water pollution problems all over the world. The Corps is now working hard on proposals to avoid, not solve, these problems by building pipelines for miles beside rivers, even the James, or southwest to a North Carolina lake, threading through several polluted rivers to find enough clean water to supply the tidewater area's burgeoning population. Across the Elizabeth, the Corps' dredging of ship channels goes on, daily adding acres of sediment to that already accumulated and named Craney Island. The skyline of the entire area is punctuated by cranes of metal, not those which fly gracefully over natural wetlands. One expert warned us of the dangers to fish and waterfowl from the disturbance of polluted sediments, and yet another argued for even deeper dredging in the river and the Roads to accommodate larger ships.

As we sailed up the James, we passed the busy docks of Newport News, where waterborne energy and defense are still linked. Miles of railroad cars empty upriver coal into huge colliers which float beside the abandoned USS *United States*, two natural gas carriers, and many "sturgeon-class" submarines being repaired or built. We were assaulted by a barrage of statistics—how many tons, how quickly loaded, how deep, but mostly how much money and how many jobs are connected with this port.

In the foreground, though, were a few small fishing boats flying yellow flags, each with two watermen repeatedly tonging clams and oysters from a river contaminated primarily by area human wastes. We were assured that the day's catch would be moved under guard to cleaner waters for two weeks of self-purification before they would be sold. Meanwhile, we listened to plans for improving the treatment of local sewage, keeping a careful watch on the release of toxic amounts of chlorine into the estuary. Dealing with the river's increasing load of human waste is another battle but one with few victories, easily nullified by the next heavy rainfall or upstream industrial or residential development.

As we passed under the James River bridge, the tidewater link between the urbanized north side of the river and the smaller towns and farms on the south, we formally entered the river. Our propellers met none of the heaps of giant oysters many feet high which once blocked colonial ships. Instead, the dredge we dropped to scrape rocks with names given centuries ago scooped up relatively small oysters, the brood stock and their young or spat, which have fastened on piles of old shells in this nursery of the Bay. Depleted by disease, pollution, and harvesting, these oysters still seem determined to reproduce, right here and nowhere else, while marine biologists work against the clock to unravel the complications of their life cycles and counteract their vulnerability. What we did not see are the underwater grasses

Aerial view of Newport News Shipbuilding and Dry Dock Company installation. Above are coal loading facilities. Ships lie at anchor, top right, waiting to take on coal. —*Richmond Newspapers*

which once sheltered baby crabs and other nursery animals but have now succumbed to too much "nutrient enrichment" from upstream fertilizer runoff and sewage effluent.

Finally the boat maneuvered through the narrow entrance to Deep Creek, a small harbor lined by marshland which is peacefully shared by both working boats and pleasure craft. The imposing riverfront houses took on a somewhat menacing air, however, as we were told the fate of miles of similar wetlands, now lost to drainage and filling, the victims of an understandable human desire to be physically close to water, at almost any price. As a biologist warned, the nursery wetlands and thus the river and the Bay could be slowly loved to death.

We heard a few answers that day, but more good questions and troublesome issues. The paradox of the naming struck me most, however. Here were experts, armed with statistics and detailed, almost esoteric knowledge about one particular aspect of the river, unable to see far beyond their own intellectual and political territory. Yet together they had managed to project for us a new vision of the river and the Bay as a totally connected web of life, sensitive to and essential for human activity. We might disagree on certain issues, and some did, in friendly conversation. But no one was disagreeing about the ultimate goal of restoring the life of the Bay, or the fact that every person living upstream in a river basin will have to assume some responsibility to keep "their" river healthy. As one Southside supervisor, long a resident beside the James, admitted, "I guess I never really understood about rivers before." So progresses a rather quiet revolution.

The day of talking was done, and as we sailed toward a Newport News dock, I watched the river silently, also seeing it in a new way. It was not so much the water life that I was picturing, however, as the reflected faces of all those people who have taught me different ways to understand and name the river for the past few years. Some were even standing

Summer, Richmond: Enjoying the river. —*Richmond Newspapers*

beside me at the railing, watching the James River bridge recede into the setting sun. Many are professionals who spend much of their time battling for, not against, the river so that their neighbors can share this "resource" without harming it or themselves. Under all their precise words and numbers, frustration and conflict, I keep discovering shared feelings for this historic river, inadequately named by words like "fascination," "respect," even "love." This river's future, they assure me, will be different from its past. I trust that other American rivers will be as fortunate in their caretakers.

Looking upstream along the lengthening rays of the sun, I traced out the shape of the river in my mind. Once what I saw was a ribbon of sometimes muddy water, falling to the Bay between walls of green trees and golden fields, or a thinning blue line weaving across the landscape of a map. The water, land, and people seemed to be separated entities, touching only on their edges.

The river I now see cannot be that easily drawn. It stretches over a wide basin in a network of streams which circulates through and over the earth and the bodies of living creatures, joining them forever. There are few lines or edges, and no stillness to be found, only multitudes of fluid connections, renewed and reconciled through the ceaseless movement of water answering the call of gravity. Time means little in this world without beginnings or endings, where there are only the tireless changes of unaltering cycles.

Each drop of the river contains and mirrors the whole. Somewhere, high in the Alleghenies, a raindrop is sliding from an oak leaf into a rockbound creek to begin its rambunctious trek to the sea. In previous incarnations it could have flowed in any river in the world, but today it becomes the river James. It will carry and discard much before it reaches the river's mouth—soil, bacteria, chemicals, trash—and it may squeeze through the cells of insects, fish, or people. Perhaps at one point it will detour through me and clear my vision in a blink. As it flows, it will repeatedly risk early liberation into the air by the sun, but even then it may return swiftly in the dew. Eventually, riding the currents and tides, it will lose itself in a burden of salt, and wait for its turn on the beach.

Never before has this drop—and its river—been so exhaustively analyzed and defined. Yet we may be seeing the river today through a mosaic of a broken lens, each piece projecting a focused but slightly different picture, and not one showing enough. To fit them together, we must acknowledge that finally the river—miracle of renewal, constancy, and equilibrium—cannot be completely named, managed, or owned. All our accumulating knowlege must be tempered by the wise ignorance which knows that the ways and rhythms of the river, like those of our lives, sometimes reach beyond the limits of our understanding. When the river loses its freedom to run freely, to be itself, usually it is we who eventually lose.

As the sun drops, my mind goes to another sunset, many miles upstream, which silhouetted no machines or ships, only the river's mineral-streaked rock sculpture against the sounds of rapids and birds. No matter where I go on this river, this spot will remain in memory my special place of balancing and letting go. Here I forget what I know about rivers so that I can see the seamless river time which promises perpetual beginnings in the midst of entropy. The river is a riddle which will never be answered by words like "hydrologic cycle," "millions of gallons per day," nor by any of the names I have gathered. Language, numbers, and even metaphors serve for what they are, partial records of what we have seen at different times and places that show how we keep taming our rivers with words. But beyond them there is time and silence—and the inexplicable spirit of the river.

SOURCES CONSULTED

Afloat on the James. New York: Giles Company, 1890s. Virginia Navigation Company.

Amos, William H. *The Infinite River: A Biologist's Vision of the World of Water.* New York: Random House, 1970.

Atran, Steven, J. G. Loesch, W. H. Kriete, and Ben Rizzo. *Feasibility Study of Fish Passage Facilities in the James River. Richmond, Va.* Gloucester Point, Va.: Virginia Institute of Marine Sciences, 1983.

Bagby, George W. *Reminiscences: Recollections of Travel in the Old Days on the James River and Kanawha Canal.* Richmond: West, Johnson & Co., 1879.

Baker, M. N. *The Quest for Pure Water.* New York: American Water Works Association, 1948.

Barbour, Philip L. "The First Reconnaissance of the James." *Virginia Cavalcade,* 17 (Autumn 1967), 35–41.

Barbour, Philip L., editor. *The Jamestown Voyages under the First Charter, 1606–1609.* Two volumes. Cambridge: University Press, 1969.

Barbour, Philip L. *Pocahontas and Her World.* Boston: Houghton Mifflin Co., 1970.

Barbour, Philip L. *The Three Worlds of Captain John Smith.* Boston: Houghton Mifflin Co., 1964.

Bardach, John. *Downstream: A Natural History of the River.* New York: Harper and Row, 1964.

Beatty, Richmond C. *William Byrd of Westover.* Boston: Houghton Mifflin Co., 1932.

Beatty, Richmond C., and William J. Mulloy. *William Byrd's Natural History of Virginia.* Richmond: Dietz Press, 1940.

Bell, M. A., et al. *Reviews of the Environmental Effects of Pollutants. I. Mirex and Kepone.* Washington, D.C.: Environmental Protection Agency (Report No. 600), July 1978.

Berry, Thomas S. "The Rise of Flour Milling in Richmond." *Virginia Magazine of History and Biography,* 78 (October 1970), 386–408.

Beverley, Robert. *The History and Present State of Virginia.* Edited by Louis B. Wright. Chapel Hill: University of North Carolina Press, 1947.

Blake, Nelson M. *Water for the Cities: A History of the Urban Water Supply Problem in the United States.* Syracuse: Syracuse University Press, 1956.

Boyle, Robert H. *The Hudson River: A Natural and Unnatural History.* New York: Norton, 1969.

Brandon, William. *The Last Americans: The Indian in American Culture.* New York: McGraw-Hill, 1974.

Brauer, Ernest. *Living Water.* Palo Alto: American-Western Publishing Co., 1971.

Breen, T. H. *Puritans and Adventurers: Change and Persistence in Early America.* New York, Oxford: Oxford University Press, 1980.

Brehmer, Morris L., and S. O. Haltiwanger. *A Biological and Chemical Study of the Tidal James River.* Gloucester Point, Va.: Virginia Institute of Marine Sciences (Special Science Report No. 6), 15 November 1966.

Bridenbaugh, Carl. *Jamestown, 1544–1699.* New York: Oxford University Press, 1980.

Brittain, Robert. *Rivers, Man and Myths: From Fish Spears to Water Mills.* Garden City: Doubleday & Co., 1958.

Brown, Alexander, editor. *Genesis of the United States.* Two volumes. New York: Russell and Russell, 1964 (1890).

Brunsdeu, Denys, John C. Doornkamp, and D. Ingle-Smith. *The Unquiet Landscape.* New York: John Wiley & Sons, 1975.

Bugg, James L., Jr. "The French Huguenot Frontier Settlement of Manakin Town," *Virginia Magazine of History and Biography,* 61 (October 1953), 303–394.

Bullington, Ann. *Vignettes of the James.* Richmond: Richmond Press, 1941.

Bushnell, David I., Jr. *The Five Monacan Towns in Virginia, 1607.* Washington, D.C.: Smithsonian, 1930.

Bushnell, David I., Jr. "Virginia Before Jamestown." Washington, D.C.: Smithsonian, 1940.

"Butler's Ditch." *Virginia Cavalcade,* 14 (Spring 1965), 38–47.

Byrd, William. *The Prose Works of William Byrd of Westover.* Louis B. Wright, editor. Cambridge: Belknap, 1966.

Camp, Thomas R. *Water and Its Impurities.* New York: Reinhold, 1965.

Campbell, Charles. *History of the Colony and Ancient Dominion of Virginia.* Philadelphia: J. B. Lippincott & Co., 1860.

Cannon, Shanklin B., et al. "Epidemic Kepone Poisoning in Chemical Workers." *American Journal of Epidemiology,* 107 (1978), 529–537.

Carlson, Clarence A., and J. McCann. *River Ecology and Man: Proceedings.* Tulane: Academic Press, 1972.

Carr, Donald. *Death of the Sweet Waters.* New York: Norton, 1971.

Carter, Edward C., II, editor. *The Virginia Journals of Benjamin Henry Latrobe, 1795–1798.* Two volumes. New Haven: Yale University Press, 1977.

Catton, Bruce. *A Stillness at Appomattox.* Garden City: Doubleday & Co., 1954.

Catton, Bruce. *Terrible Swift Sword.* Garden City: Doubleday & Co., 1963.

Catton, Bruce. *This Hallowed Ground.* Garden City: Doubleday & Co., 1956.

Chesapeake Bay: Introduction to an Ecosystem. Washington, D.C.: Environmental Protection Agency, January 1982.

Chesapeake Bay Program Technical Studies: A Synthesis. Washington, D.C.: Environmental Protection Agency, September 1982.

Chesson, Michael B. *Richmond After the War, 1865–1890*. Richmond: Virginia State Library, 1981.

Chesterman, W. D. *The James River Tourist*. Richmond: Lucien B. Tatum, 1899. Sixth edition.

Chorley, Richard J., editor. *Water, Earth, and Man, A Synthesis of Hydrology, Geomorphology, and Socio-Economic Geography*. London: Methuen & Co., 1969.

Christian, W. Asbury. *Lynchburg and Its People*. Lynchburg: J. P. Bell, 1900.

Christian, W. Asbury. *Richmond, Her Past and Present*. Richmond: L. H. Jenkins, 1912.

Church, Randolph W. "Mr. Nellywood and the Querry Hole." *Virginia Cavalcade*, 4 (Summer 1954), 4–8.

Coker, Robert E. *Streams, Lakes, Ponds*. Chapel Hill: University of North Carolina Press, 1954.

Coleman, Charles. "Sturgeon Fishing in the James." *Cosmopolitan* (July 1892), 366–373.

Coleman, Elizabeth D. "The Great Fresh of 1771." *Virginia Cavalcade*, 1 (Autumn 1951), 20–22.

Conservation Council of Virginia. *Waste Alert: A Handbook for Citizens on Toxic Waste and Water Pollution Problems*. Richmond, 1982.

Corbett, H. Roger. *Virginia White Water: A Canoeing Guide to the Rivers of the Old Dominion*. New York: Seneca Press, 1977.

Couture, Richard T. *Powhatan: A Bicentennial History*. Richmond: Dietz Press, 1980.

Cox, William E., and Keith A. Argow. *Public Recreation on Virginia's Inland Streams: Legal Rights and Landowners' Perceptions*. Blacksburg, Va.: Virginia Water Resources Research Center (Bulletin 120), October 1979.

Dabney, Virginius. *Richmond: The Story of a City*. Garden City: Doubleday, 1976.

Dabney, Virginius. *Virginia, the New Dominion*. Garden City: Doubleday, 1971.

Davis, Jackson, editor. *The Effects of Tropical Storm Agnes on the Chesapeake Bay Estuarine System*. Baltimore: Johns Hopkins Press, 1977.

Deming, H. G. *Water: The Fountain of Opportunity*. New York: Oxford University Press, 1975.

Dietrich, Richard V. *Geology and Virginia*. Charlottesville: University of Virginia Press, 1970.

Dowdey, Clifford. *The Great Plantation: A Profile of Berkeley Hundred and Plantation Virginia from Jamestown to Appomattox*. Charles City, Va.: Berkeley Plantation, 1957.

Dunaway, Wayland F. *History of the James River and Kanawha Company*. New York: AMS Press, 1969.

Earle, Carville V. "Environment, Disease, and Mortality in Early Virginia" in *The Chesapeake in the Seventeenth Century: Essays on Anglo-American Society*. Thad Tate and David Ammerman, editors. Chapel Hill: University of North Carolina Press, 1979.

Eckenrode. H. J. *The Revolution in Virginia*. Hamden, Conn.: Archon Books, 1964.

Eifert, Virginia. *Of Men and Rivers*. New York: Dodd, Mead & Co., 1966.

Eiseley, Loren. *The Immense Journey*. New York: Random House, 1946.

Ekirch, Arthur E., Jr. *Man and Nature in America*. New York: Columbia University Press, 1963.

Eliade, Mircea. *Patterns in Comparative Religion*. New York: New American Library, 1974.

Evans, Cerinda. *Some Notes on Shipbuilding and Shipping in Colonial Virginia*. Williamsburg: 350th Anniversary Celebration, 1957.

Farley, Joseph Pearson. *Three Rivers: The James, The Potomac, The Hudson*. New York and Washington: The Neale Publishing Co., 1910.

Fish Commissioners of the State of Virginia. *Annual Reports, 1875–90*.

Fiske, John. *The Discovery of America*. Volume III. Boston: Houghton, Mifflin & Co., 1892.

Foote, Shelby. *The Civil War: A Narrative*. New York: Random House, 1974.

French, Herbert E. *Of Rivers and the Sea*. New York: G. P. Putnam's Sons, 1970.

Glacken, Clarence. "Changing Ideas of the Habitable World" in *Man's Role in Changing the Face of the Earth*. William L. Thomas, editor. Chicago: University of Chicago Press, 1956.

Goldenberg, Joseph A. "Virginia Ports" in *Chesapeake Bay in the American Revolution*. Ernest M. Eller, editor. Centreville, Md.: Tidewater Publishers, 1981.

Good, E. E., G. W. Ware, and D. F. Miller. "Effects of Insecticides on Reproduction in the Laboratory Mouse: I. Kepone." *J. Econ. Entomol.*, 58 (4), 754–757.

Hargis, William. *Final Report on Operation James River: An Evaluation of Physical and Biological Effects of the Proposed James River Navigation Project*. Gloucester Point, Va.: Virginia Institute of Marine Sciences, December 1966.

Hatch, Charles E., Jr. *The First Seventeen Years: Virginia, 1607–1624*. Williamsburg: Virginia 350th Anniversary Celebration Corp., 1957.

Hatch, Charles E., Jr., and T. G. Gregory. "The First American Blast Furnace, 1619–1622." *Virginia Magazine of History and Biography*, 70 (July 1962), 259–296.

Haven, Dexter, William Hargis, and Paul Kendall. *The Oyster Industry of Virginia: Its Status, Problems, and Promise*. Gloucester Point, Va.: Virginia Institute of Marine Sciences (Special Papers, No. 4), May 1978.

Heerwald, John. "Canoeing a Legend: The Fabled James." *Virginia Wildlife* (June 1983), 15–19.

Hill, Don. "Now It's that Dam Project." *The Commonwealth*, 34 (April 1967), 38–40.

Hill, Don. "Walking Along the James." Series of articles published in the Richmond *Times-Dispatch*, 1978–1979.

Horwitz, Elinor L. *Our Nation's Wetlands: An Interagency Task Force Report*. Washington: Council on Environmental Quality, 1978.

Houston, Charles. "The Troubled James." *Commonwealth*, 31 (October 1964), 23–25.

Huber, J. J. "Some Physiological Effects of the Insecticide Kepone in the Laboratory Mouse." *Toxicol. Appli. Pharmacol.* 7 (4), 516–524.

Huggett, Robert, and Michael E. Bender. "Kepone in the James River." *Environmental Science and Technology*, 14 (August 1980), 918–923.

Hume, Ivor Hoel. *Here Lies Virginia: An Archaeologist's View of Colonial Life and History*. New York: Alfred A. Knopf, 1974.

Hunt, Cynthia A., and Robert H. Garrels. *Water: The Web of Life*. New York: W. W. Norton & Co., 1972.

Hutchins, Frank, and Cortelle Hutchins. *Virginia: The Old Dominion as seen from its colonial waterway*. Boston: The Page Co., 1921.

Huth, Hans. *Nature and the American*. Berkeley: University of California Press, 1957.

Jacobs, Wilbur R. *Dispossessing the American Indian: Indians and Whites on the Colonial Frontier*. New York: Charles Scribner's Sons, 1972.

James River Basin: Comprehensive Water Resources Plan. Five volumes. Virginia Department of Conservation and Economic Development. Division of Water Resources. 1969—.

James River Corridor Study. Richmond Regional Planning District Commission, 1970s.

Jennings, Francis. *The Invasion of America: Indians, Colonialism, and the Cant of Conquest*. Chapel Hill: University of North Carolina Press, 1975.

Jensen, L. D. *Environmental Responses to Thermal Discharges from the Chesterfield Station, James River, Va*. Baltimore: Johns Hopkins, December 1974.

Jones, Howard Mumford. *O Strange New World—American Culture: The Formative Years*. New York: Viking, 1964.

Kauffman, John M. *Flow East: A Look at our North Atlantic Rivers*. New York: McGraw-Hill, 1973.

Kennedy, James Pendleton. *Swallow Barn*. New York: Hafner, 1962 (1853 edition).

Kirkwood, James J. *Waterway to the West*. Eastern National Park and Monument Association, 1963.

Klein, Frederic S. "Bottling up Butler at Bermuda Hundred." *Civil War Times Illustrated*, 6 (November 1967), 4–11, 45.

Kneese, Allen V., and Blair T. Bower. *Managing Water Quality: Economics, Technology, Institutions*. Baltimore: The Johns Hopkins Press, 1968.

Lamar, William, and George Whetstone. *Chemical Characteristics of Surface Waters of Virginia, 1945–1946*. Charlottesville: Virginia Conservation Commission, Division of Water Resources and Power, 1947.

Leopold, Luna. *Fluvial Processes in Geomorphology*. San Francisco: W. H. Freeman, 1964.

Leopold, Luna B. *Water, A Primer*. San Francisco: W. H. Freeman, 1974.

Lewis, Ronald. *Coal, Iron, and Slaves: Industrial Slavery in Maryland and Virginia, 1755–1865*. Westport, Conn.: Greenwood Press, 1979.

Lunsford, C. A., C. L. Walton, and J. W. Shell. *Summary of Kepone Study Results—1976–1978*. Richmond: Virginia State Water Control Board, January 1980.

Lurie, Nancy O. "Indian Cultural Adjustment to European Civilization" in *Seventeenth-Century America*. James M. Smith, editor. Chapel Hill: University of North Carolina Press, 1959.

Lutz, Francis E. *Chesterfield: An Old Virginia County*. Richmond: William Byrd Press, 1954.

Lutz, Francis E. *The Prince George–Hopewell Story*. Richmond: William Byrd Press, 1957.

McCary, Ben C. *Indians in Seventeenth Century Virginia*. Williamsburg: Virginia 350th Anniversary Celebration Corp., 1957.

McPherson, James M. *Ordeal by Fire: The Civil War and Reconstruction*. New York: Alfred A. Knopf, 1982.

Mann, Roy. *Rivers in the City*. New York: Praeger, 1973.

Marine, Gene. *America the Raped: The Engineering Mentality and the Devastation of a Continent*. New York: Simon & Schuster, 1969.

Marsh, George Perkins. *Man and Nature*. David Lowenthal, editor. Cambridge: Belknap Press, 1965 (1874).

Marx, Leo. *The Machine in the Garden: Technology and the Pastoral Ideal in America*. New York: Oxford University Press, 1964.

Massmann, William H., and Robert S. Bailey. "Virginia's Anadromous Fishes." *Virginia Wildlife* (April 1961).

Maurey, Richard P. *The Huguenots in Virginia*. Reprinted from the Memorial Volumes of the Huguenot Society of America. N.p., n.d.

Michener, James A. *Chesapeake*. New York: Random House, 1978.

Milne, Lorus, and Margery Milne. *Water and Life*. New York: Atheneum, 1972.

Mitchell, Lee Clark. *Witnesses to a Vanishing America: The Nineteenth Century Response*. Princeton: Princeton University Press, 1981.

Mooney, James. "The Powhatan Confederacy, Past and Present." *American Anthropologist*, 9 (January-March 1907), 129–152.

Moore, Virginia. *Scottsville on the James*. Charlottesville: The Jarman Press, 1969.

Mordecai, Samuel. *Richmond in By-gone Days*. Richmond: Dietz Press, 1940. Reprint of 2nd edition, 1860.

Morgan, William J. "Torpedoes in the James." *The Iron Worker*, 26 (Summer 1962), 1–11.

Morisawa, Marie. *Streams: Their Dynamics and Morphology*. New York: McGraw-Hill, 1968.

Mouer, L. Daniel. "Powhatan and Monacan Regional Settlement Hierarchies: A Model of Relationship Between Social and Environmental Structure." *Quarterly Bulletin of the Archeological Society of Virginia*, 36 (September 1981), 1–21.

Mouer, L. Daniel, Robin L. Ryder, and Elizabeth G. Johnson. "Down to the River in Boats: The Late Archaic/Transitional in the Middle James River Valley, Virginia." *Quarterly Bulletin of the Archeological Society of Virginia*, 36 (September 1981), 29–48.

Mouer, L. Daniel, Robin L. Ryder, and Elizabeth G. Johnson. "The Elk Island Tradition: An Early Woodland Regional Society in The Virginia Piedmont." *Quarterly Bulletin of the Archeological Society of Virginia*, 36 (September 1981), 49–76.

Nash, Roderick. *The American Environment: Readings in the History of Conservation*. 2nd edition. Reading, Mass.: Addison-Wesley, 1968.

Nash, Roderick. *Wilderness and the American Mind*. Revised edition. New Haven: Yale University Press, 1973.

Neilson, Bruce J., and Penelope S. Ferry. *A Water Quality Study of the Estuarine James River*. Gloucester Point, Va.: Virginia Institute of Marine Sciences (SRAMSOE 131), January 1978.

Nevins, Allan. *The War for the Union*. Volume II. New York: Charles Scribner's Sons, 1960.

Niles, Blair. *The James: From Iron Gate to the Sea*. New York: Rinehart & Co., 1945.

Nye, Russel B. *This Almost Chosen People: Essays in the History of American Ideas*. East Lansing: Michigan State University Press, 1966.

Paine, Lauran. *Captain John Smith and the Jamestown Story*. London: Robert Hale, 1973.

Parker, Frank, and Peter Krinkel. *Engineering Aspects of Thermal Pollution*. Nashville: Vanderbilt University Press, 1961.

Parker, G. C., and C. S. Fang. *Thermal Effects of the Surry Nuclear Power Plant on the James River, Virginia*. Gloucester Point, Va.: Virginia Institute of Marine Sciences, 1975–1976.

Patrick, Rembert W. *The Fall of Richmond*. Baton Rouge: Louisiana State University Press, 1960.

Pearce, Roy Harvey. *Savagism and Civilization: A Study of the Indian and the American Mind*. Baltimore: Johns Hopkins University Press, 1965.

Perlman, Stephen M. "Hunter-Gatherer Social Systems and the James River Middle Archaic Lithic Utilization." *Quarterly Bulletin of the Archeological Society of Virginia*, 36 (September 1981), 22–28.

Peters, John M. "The Kepone Episode: Another Warning." *The New England Journal of Medicine*, 298 (February 2, 1978), 277–278.

Pollution and Its Control on the James River from Richmond to the Bay: Report of the National Wildlife Federation to the Virginia Environmental Endowment. Washington, D.C.: National Wildlife Federation, July 1981.

Powledge, Fred. *Water: The Nature, Uses, and Future of Our Most Precious and Abused Resource*. New York: Farrar Straus Giroux, 1982.

Regenstein, Lewis. *America the Poisoned.* Washington, D.C.: Acropolis Books, 1982.

Richmond/Crater 208 Interim Water Quality Management Plan. Richmond: Virginia State Water Control Board, December 1982.

Richmond *Times-Dispatch.* Numerous articles.

Richmond, Virginia, The City on the James: The Book of Its Chamber of Commerce and Principal Business Interests. Richmond: George W. Engelhardt, 1902–1903.

Robbinson, William M., Jr. "Drewry's Bluff: Naval Defense of Richmond, 1862." *Civil War History,* 7 (June 1961), 167–175.

Rouse, Parke, Jr. *Below the James Lies Dixie.* Richmond: The Dietz Press, 1968.

Rubin, Louis, Jr. *Virginia: A Bicentennial History.* New York: Norton, 1977.

Ryan, David. *The Falls of the James.* Richmond: William Byrd Press, 1975.

The Saga of a City: Lynchburg, Virginia, 1786–1936. Lynchburg: Sesquicentennial Association, 1936.

Schoenbaum, Thomas J. *The New River Controversy.* Winston-Salem, N.C.: John F. Blair, 1979.

Scribner, Robert L. "Belle Isle." *Virginia Cavalcade,* 5 (Winter 1955), 8–14.

Sears, Paul B. "The Processes of Environmental Change by Man," in *Man's Role in Changing the Face of the Earth.* William L. Thomas, editor. Chicago: University of Chicago Press, 1956.

Seelye, John. *Prophetic Waters: The River in Early American Life and Literature.* New York: Oxford University Press, 1977.

Sheehan, Bernard W. *Savagism and Civility: Indians and Englishmen in Colonial Virginia.* Cambridge: Cambridge University Press, 1980.

Smith, Bradford. *Captain John Smith: His Life and Legend.* Philadelphia: J. B. Lippincott Co., 1953.

Smith, Henry Nash. *Virgin Land: The American West as Symbol and Myth.* New York: Random House, 1950.

Smith, John. *Captain John Smith's History of Virginia: A Selection.* David F. Hawke, editor. Indianapolis: Bobbs-Merrill, 1970.

Stanard, Mary Newton. *Richmond, Its People and Its Story.* Philadelphia: J. B. Lippincott, 1923.

Stanard, Mary Newton. *The Story of Virginia's First Century.* Philadelphia: J. B. Lippincott, 1928.

Sterrett, Frances S., and Caroline A. Boss. "Careless Kepone." *Environment,* 19 (March 1977), 30–37.

Stevens, Leonard A. *Clean Water, Nature's Way to Stop Pollution.* New York: E. P. Dutton, 1974.

Stewart, Robert Armistead. *The History of Virginia's Navy of the Revolution.* Richmond: Mitchell and Hotchkiss, 1933.

Stith, William. *The History and the First Discovery and Settlement of Virginia.* Williamsburg, 1747. Reprinted by Heritage Series, Spartanburg, S.C.

Teal, John, and Mildred Teal. *Life and Death of the Salt Marsh.* New York: Ballantine Books, 1969.

Thomas, Bill. *American Rivers: A Natural History*. New York: W. W. Norton, 1978.

Thomas, Emory M. *The Confederate State of Richmond*. Austin: University of Texas Press, 1971.

Thomas, William L., editor. *Man's Role in Changing the Face of the Earth*. Chicago: University of Chicago Press, 1956.

Thoreau, Henry David. *The River: Selections from the Journal of Henry David Thoreau*. Dudley C. Lunt, arranger. New York: Twayne Publishers, 1963.

Thoreau, Henry David. *Walden*. J. Lyndon Shanley, editor. Princeton: Princeton University Press, 1971.

Thoreau, Henry David. *A Week on the Concord and Merrimack Rivers*. Carl F. Hovde, editor. Princeton: Princeton University Press, 1980.

Tichi, Cecelia. *New World, New Earth: Environmental Reform in American Literature from the Puritans through Whitman*. New Haven: Yale University Press, 1979.

Twain, Mark (Samuel Clemens). *Life on the Mississippi*. New York: The Franklin Library, 1981.

Tyler, Lyon G., editor. *Narratives of Early Virginia*. New York: Barnes and Noble, 1907.

Udall, Stewart L. *The Quiet Crisis*. New York: Avon, 1963.

Usinger, Robert. *The Life of Rivers and Streams*. New York: McGraw-Hill, 1967.

Vaughan, Alden T. *American Genesis: Captain John Smith and the Founding of Virginia*. Boston: Little, Brown & Co., 1975.

Virginia Academy of Science. *James River Basin: Past, Present, and Future*. Richmond, 1950.

Walker, William. *Flood Damage Abatement Study for Virginia*. Blacksburg, Va.: Virginia Water Resources Research Center (Bulletin 10), 1971.

Walker, William R., and William E. Cox. *Water Resources Administration in Virginia: Analysis and Evaluation*. Blacksburg, Va.: Virginia Water Resources Research Center (Bulletin 107), December 1976.

Ward, Christopher. *The War of the Revolution*. New York: Macmillan Company, 1952.

Ward, Harry M., and Harold E. Greer, Jr. *Richmond During the Revolution, 1775–83*. Charlottesville: University Press of Virginia, 1977.

Warner, William W. *Beautiful Swimmers: Watermen, Crabs and the Chesapeake Bay*. Boston: Little, Brown & Co., 1976.

Washburn, Wilcomb E. *The Indian in America*. New York: Harper and Row, 1975.

Wharton, James. *The Bounty of the Chesapeake: Fishing in Colonial Virginia*. Williamsburg: Virginia 350th Anniversary Celebration Corp., 1957.

Whisenhunt, Donald W. *The Environment and the American Experience: A Historian Looks at the Ecological Crisis*. Port Washington, N.Y.: The Kennikat Press, 1974.

White, Gilbert F. *Strategies of·American Water Management*. Ann Arbor: University of Michigan, 1969.

SOURCES CONSULTED

White, Lynn, Jr. "The Historical Roots of Our Ecologic Crisis." *Science*, 155 (10 March 1967), 1203–1207.

(Woodrow, Fred). Wor Doow. *The James River or Rhymes, Legendary and Historical, of "The Old Powhatan."* Claremont, Virginia: Claremont *Herald*, 1889.

Virginia Hydro Dam Inventory. Volume II—South Atlantic Slope. Afton, Va.: Rockfish Corp. (Virginia State Office of Emergency and Energy Sources), August 1981.

INDEX

66, 73; legendary, 147–48; modern, 158, 203, 206–8. *See also*
Civil War; ferries; ironclads;
James River and Kanawha Canal;
navigation; packet boats; Revolutionary War; shipbuilding
Bosher Dam, 110, 115–16, 137
Brim, 197
Broad Rock Island. *See* Belle Isle
Buchanan, 1, 97, 104, 202; and
canal, 99–101
Bullington, Ann, 174
Burke, Louise, 200–201
Burroughs, John, 139
Burwell's Ferry, 93
Butler, General Benjamin, 135–36, 166
Byrd, William I, 74, 82–83, 84, 117–18
Byrd, William II, 74–75, 84–85, 113, 115, 117–18, 206
Byrd, William III, 75, 87, 117–18

Campbell, Charles, 68–69, 91
Canals, 85, 87, 95–104, 112–13, 118–20, 135–36, 152, 156, 158, 167–68, 170. *See also* James
River Canal; James River and
Kanawha Canal; Manchester
Cape Henry, 35
Capitol (Virginia), 102, 148, 152
Carson, Rachel, 184
Carter, Robert (King), 77
Cartier, Jacques, 31
Caruthers, William A., 139, 140–41
Catton, Bruce, 129
Cavalier of Virginia, or the Recluse of Jamestown, The, 140–41
Cavaliers, 67, 91, 140
Caviar. *See* sturgeon
Chaffin's Bluff, 130
Channelization, 176–77
Charles City County, 78–79
"Chemical Character of Surface
Waters of Virginia, 1945–1946,"
162–63
Chemical industry, 160–64, 183–84, 189–90, 207. *See also* Hercules; Allied; Kepone
Chesapeake and Ohio Railroad, 157

Chesapeake Bay, 2, 12–14, 17–18, 44–45, 47, 58, 73, 76, 157, 198, 206–8; early explorations of, 33–35, 45–48. *See also* Kepone;
Chesapeake Bay study
Chesapeake Bay study, 194–95, 207–8, 210
Chesterman, William, 148
Chickahominy River, 14, 45–46, 47, 49, 130–31, 148
Chlorine, 194, 208
Cholestyramine, 190
Church Hill, 134. *See also*
Richmond
City Point, 135, 136
Civil War (War Between the States), 78, 101, 102, 128–38, 152, 157
Clams, 174, 208
Claremont *Herald,* 144, 147
Clean Water Act, 185
Clean Water Campaign, 184
"Cleaning the James," 170
Clinton, General Henry, 93
College of William and Mary, 76
Commission of Game and Inland
Fisheries (Va.), 184, 202
Commodore Barney (USS), 131
Commodore Jones (USS), 131–32, 135
Concord River, 150
Congress (USS), 129
Continental Congress, 77
Cooke, G., 152
Cooke, John Esten, 139, 141–42
Corn: Indian, 19, 24, 45, 49–50, 53, 84, 112; whiskey, 101
Cornwallis, General Charles, 93–94
Cousteau, Jacques, 207
Cowpasture River, 10
Crabs, 187–88, 194–95, 199, 210
Craney Island, 208
Cranstone, Lefevre J., 150
CSX Corporation, 102–3
Cumberland (USS), 129
Curles Neck, 68
Currier and Ives, 150

Dabney, Virginius, 84
Dahlgren, Colonel Ulrich, 134–35
Dale, Sir Thomas, 66–67
Dams, 4, 58, 97, 110, 114, 121,

In River Time has been composed in Bembo on a Merganthaler Linotron 202 by G&S Typesetters of Austin, Texas. The text has been printed on 60 pound P&S Smooth Offset and bound in Iris 101 by Mapel-Vail Book Manufacturing of Binghamton, New York. The sixteen page insert has been printed on 80 pound Lustro Offset Dull Cream by Rapaport Printing Corporation of New York City. This book was designed and produced by Anne Theilgard of Joyce Kachergis Book Design & Production of Bynum, North Carolina.